A Woman's Path to Emotional Freedom

Julie Clinton

HARVEST HOUSE PUBLISHERS

EUGENE, OREGON

Cover by Koechel Peterson & Associates, Inc., Minneapolis, Minnesota

Cover photo © Photos.com

This book includes stories in which the author has changed people's names and some details of their situations to protect their privacy.

A WOMAN'S PATH TO EMOTIONAL FREEDOM
Copyright © 2010 by Julie Clinton
Published by Harvest House Publishers
Eugene, Oregon 97402
www.harvesthousepublishers.com

Library of Congress Cataloging-in-Publication Data
    Clinton, Julie
    A woman's path to emotional freedom / Julie Clinton.
        p. cm.
    ISBN 978-0-7369-2996-7 (pbk.)
    1. Christian women—Religious life. 2. Emotions—Religious aspects—Christianity. I.
Title.
    BV4527.C573 2010
    248.8'43—dc22
                                                            2009052332

Printed in the United States of America

10 11 12 13 14 15 16 17 18 / VP-SK / 10 9 8 7 6 5 4 3 2 1

My heart goes out to you, and I long to see you all
coming constantly to God for a fresh supply of love.

D.L. MOODY

This book is dedicated to the special women in my life—
my mother, Marylin Rothmann, my sister, Jana Queen,
and my beautiful daughter, Megan Ann—along with all
of the precious women of our Extraordinary Women staff,
members of the Extraordinary Women Association, and
conference attendees. May you always be able to transcend
your pain and overcome obstacles for the glory of God!

Acknowledgments

*The next best thing to being wise oneself
is to live in a circle of those who are.*
C.S. LEWIS

I am blessed and thankful to my heavenly Father for giving me an enormous circle of dear colleagues and cherished friends who are faithful every day to seek his wisdom and direction for their lives. I wish to acknowledge and thank them for the love and support they have shown to me in the completion of this manuscript.

A special thank you to Pat Springle for his help in writing this book. Pat, you have always been willing to share godly wisdom and your gift of writing with me, and I am truly appreciative of the hard work you have put into making this book special.

Extending a heartfelt and sincere thank-you to Harvest House Publishers doesn't seem enough for the support and encouragement they have given to me over the years, but here goes—thank you, Carolyn McCready, Gene Skinner, and the entire Harvest House staff, for giving me this opportunity to share my heart and help women across the world find freedom from emotional pain.

Once again, my sincerest thanks goes to Dr. Joshua Straub, Amy Feigel, and Laura Faidley for the editing expertise, research, and insight they provided throughout the entire book. You guys are great!

And of course, to the "E-Team"—thank you for dedicating long hours during the week and on the weekends to faithfully serve Christ and women across this nation. I am grateful and feel extremely blessed to serve with you!

Tim, Megan, and Zach—I thank God every day for the blessing you are in my life. You mean more to me than anything in this world. God has taught me so much about emotional stability through each of you. Thank you for your patience when my emotions occasionally get the best of me!

Contents

Introduction

Windows into a Woman's Heart

Your beauty should not come from outward
adornment...Instead, it should be that of your inner
self, the unfading beauty of a gentle and quiet spirit,
which is of great worth in God's sight. For this is
the way the holy women of the past who put their
hope in God used to make themselves beautiful

1 PETER 3:3-5

You may be naturally beautiful. I'm not. It takes a little work to get this girl up, dressed, and out the door.

Some mornings I love getting ready. Other mornings, I loathe it. You know what I'm talking about—the princess in you loves dolling herself up before the ball, but the cranky "I don't want to be up this early" part of you wishes you could stay in bed a little longer (like your husband does).

On the good mornings, I especially love doing my eyes. My husband, Tim (who happens to be a counselor), thinks it must have started when I was little. Maybe someone made fun of my eyes sometime when I was younger. I can't remember, but for some reason I have always been intrigued with dressing them with just the right amount of mascara, liner, and color.

I'm also intrigued by the makeup ladies in the department stores. They enjoy helping women find just the right shades. When a store isn't busy, I have seen them experimenting on each other and trying new products on themselves. Tim, however, isn't quite as fascinated with cosmetics as I am. He doesn't even stop. When I slow down, he walks right past me with a quick smile and grunts, "I'll be in the men's department."

A few minutes with the girls in the cosmetics section is like caffeine to me. I can shop all day!

Through the years I have grown to notice the eyes of other women as well. People's eyes fascinate me because they are among the most expressive parts of the body. We work to highlight the beauty God has given us, hide wrinkles, cover bags when we're tired, and mask blemishes. But regardless of how much makeup we use, our eyes express more than physical beauty. They also reveal what's going on inside us emotionally. No wonder our eyes are often called the windows into our souls.

With only a quick glance or perhaps a longing gaze, women communicate and sometimes scream powerful messages. For example, I have looked at women's eyes and seen...

- joy when they heard good news
- peace and contentment when they trusted God's goodness, wisdom, and strength in the midst of turmoil
- genuine kindness when they empathized with their friends' joys and losses
- passionate love when they saw their husbands or fiancés (and I trust Tim has seen this look in my eyes)

But I've also looked at women's eyes and seen...

- seductive looks when they wanted forbidden men
- anger and even uncontrolled rage when they felt terribly wronged
- deep sorrow and sometimes hopelessness when they couldn't see any way forward

- envy when they believed they deserved the blessings others enjoy

And far too often, I've looked in the mirror after a particularly hectic day to see the eyes of someone who is simply exhausted.

Of course, the looks in our eyes are so subtle and expressive that we communicate a thousand variations of these not-so-hidden messages. Some of us are almost clairvoyant in our ability to read people's expressions. With only a glance into their eyes, we instantly know exactly what they're thinking and feeling. But to be candid, others of us are clueless. We look, but we don't see. The person in front of us is like a beautiful, inspiring, insightful book sitting on the table in arm's length, but we don't even open the first page.

My eyes are an ocean
in which my dreams are reflected.
ANONYMOUS

In a 1978 Gallup poll, people were asked if a series of qualities applied more to men or to women. Ninety percent of American adults said that women are more emotional than men.[1]

Are women more emotional than men? The perception is common. Interestingly, as infants, boys and girls cry about the same amount. But once girls hit puberty, they begin crying a whole lot more than boys. So much more that by age 18, young women are crying four times more than young men.[2] Maybe men stuff their feelings, and we women just feel and express them more. And as part of this journey, we are sometimes emotional wrecks. When I am, Tim runs, and the dogs hide under the bed (not really). More often than not we take a while to understand what's behind our feelings. Sometimes we don't care; we just need time to do our thing. At other times, we are blind to what is going on inside of us, or we simply lie to ourselves. And far too often, we let our emotions run our lives. Would you agree?

Our Eyes Speak Volumes

In 1955, Joseph Luft and Harry Ingham pulled their names together to label the Johari Window, a psychological tool that describes people's interpersonal communications and relationships. The person doing the exercise reads a list of fifty-five adjectives and chooses five or six that she believes describe her own personality. Then, friends and family choose five or six adjectives that describe that person. Once the adjectives are chosen, they are mapped onto a grid like the one shown below.

Things I know about myself	Things I don't know about myself
my public self	my blind spots
my hidden self	my unconscious self

FIGURE 1. THE JOHARI WINDOW

The public self includes the traits that we know about ourselves and that others know about us. When people first meet us, this window is almost empty. As our relationships progress, more and more information becomes available to others.

The blind spots are the things that others know about us but that we don't know about ourselves. They are like pieces of broccoli stuck in our teeth. For example, we may not realize that our tendency to be inflexible keeps our friends from inviting us out on a girls' night.

The hidden self is made up of things we know about ourselves that others do not know. Rarely will we share parts of ourselves until we trust others.

Finally, the unconscious self contains things that neither we nor others know about us. When we discuss a dream we had or talk about why we are so shy around a particular group of people, we discover new parts of our personalities.

How do your emotions fit into the Johari Window? You and your friends are very aware of some of your emotions, like your anger toward a rebellious teenager or the happiness of receiving flowers from your husband. You are also very aware of some emotions that you keep secret, like the deep sadness you feel about your husband working all of the time. You can't see some of your emotions that others can see, such as when you yell at your children a little too much because you are angry at your own parents for treating you so poorly.

Over the past couple of years, I've talked to thousands of women who have experienced more than their share of trials, hurt, and confusion. And sometimes I've been in the same boat. Some of us are quite aware of the pain we feel. In fact, the constant and gnawing hurt clouds much of our lives. But many of us have become skilled at avoiding or masking our pain from a bad marriage, an abusive past, put-downs at work, loss, or gossip. We tell ourselves, *It wasn't that bad*, or *He couldn't help it*, or *It didn't happen at all*. But it did, and it hurt terribly.

Trying to deny our pain only causes it to smolder under the surface until it eventually explodes in deep anger or implodes in depression. Even when we try to suppress our damaged emotions, our eyes tell the real story.

> There is a road from the eye to heart that does not go through the intellect.
>
> G.K. CHESTERTON

Things Aren't Always as They Seem

I remember hearing a story about a 23-year-old woman named Linda. While visiting her in-laws one weekend, Linda made a quick trip to a grocery store to pick up a few things for dinner. Many people saw her sitting in the grocery-store parking lot with her hands behind her head and her eyes closed. Finally, a man saw her when he was walking in the store and again 30 minutes later when he was walking out. She hadn't moved, so he decided to make sure she was okay.

Tap, tap, tap…He knocked on the driver's side window.

"Are you okay?" he yelled.

Without moving her hands, she shook her head no. "I've been shot…" she mouthed back to him.

Immediately the man called 9-1-1.

Paramedics rushed to the scene and asked Linda to unlock her doors, but she refused in fear of taking her hands off the back of her head. After breaking into the car through the passenger's side window, they began to investigate what happened.

"I was shot, and I've been sitting here holding the back of my head together," she said tearfully.

As the police and paramedics continued investigating the situation, they discovered no bullet holes in the car at all. Instead, they found an empty Pillsbury bread dough canister lying in the backseat. The canister had apparently exploded in the heat of the sun, making a loud noise like a gunshot and sending the bread dough straight into the back of Linda's head. She lost consciousness for a brief moment, quickly regained it, felt the back of her head, and decided she should sit still and hold her brains in.

The point is that things aren't always what they seem.

The longer I live, the more I've learned to value the rare trait variously known as wisdom, insight, or perception. It's the ability to see beyond the surface and into the heart of a person or a situation. When considering spirituality, relationships, and emotional health, I don't know of any other quality that could be more valuable.

If we can see God's character and his hand clearly, we'll trust him even in our most difficult seasons of life. If we perceive others clearly, we'll know whom we can trust and when we need to be more cautious. And if we have insight about our own thoughts and feelings, we can make better choices about every aspect of our lives, from finances to family, and from sexual satisfaction to our purpose for living.

In this book we'll examine some of our emotions, wounds, and desires. We'll also examine ways we can live in a God-filled reality every day. From the outset, I want to make it clear that our emotions are indicators of our present inward condition. Even the most painful emotions play an important role in driving us to God to trust him for comfort and direction.

Author Philip Yancey partnered with physician Paul Brand to write their insightful book *The Gift of Pain*. Brand was an orthopedic surgeon working with leprosy patients in India. As Yancey observed Brand at work with his patients, he realized that the biggest problems associated with this dreaded disease were caused by the *absence* of pain. When people with the disease don't feel the heat of a flame, they burn their fingers. When they don't feel the pain of other injuries, infection often causes them to lose body parts. Yancey concluded that pain is the language that alerts the person of a danger or need. In the same way, wise women recognize pain as the flashing red light on the dashboard of their lives that warns them that something needs attention. We may want to live free from all anger, sorrow, or fear, but that's not the way God designed life to work. Every kind of pain is a gift from God, and we are wise to pay attention to it.

Is it wrong to be angry? Not always. Is it wrong to be scared? Not always. Is it wrong to feel sad? Of course not! Feeling angry, fearful, or sad is not wrong. But the ways we respond to and act out that anger, fear, or sadness can be helpful or hurtful. Denying our feelings, suppressing them, trying to act like nothing happened, allowing the experience to fuel the desire to take revenge against somebody...these things are wrong. Instead, we need to attend to these negative feelings by setting healthy boundaries, speaking the truth, and courageously moving forward with our lives.

If we clearly recognize our emotions (both painful and pleasant) and respond appropriately, we can prevent a lot of personal heartache for us and for those we love. Jesus taught that the way we perceive our world makes all the difference: "Your eyes are windows into your body. If you open your eyes wide in wonder and belief, your body fills up with light. If you live squinty-eyed in greed and distrust, your body is a dank cellar. If you pull the blinds on your windows, what a dark life you will have!" (Matthew 6:22-23 MSG).

Jesus often used the physical world to teach a spiritual lesson. If we are blind, we stumble around and bump into all kinds of things. At best, we experience inconvenience and need others to guide us, and at worst, we feel helpless and hopeless, vulnerable to anyone who might harm us or take advantage of us.

But Jesus wasn't talking about physical blindness; he was teaching a lesson about the imperative of spiritual insight. With the clear eyes of faith, we see God more accurately—full of majesty, power, and grace. Instead of riveting our gaze on our problems, we can look beyond the obvious difficulties to see that God hasn't abandoned us. In fact, in ways we may never understand, he uses the problems in our lives to accomplish his purposes in us and through us. We know his perception is perfect, so we can trust him.

Distractions and Deceptions

Advertising dominates our world. We are enslaved to the cult of the next new thing. From all around us, we hear that we can't be satisfied unless we have this product or that service. And too often, rather than thinking about these messages, we just absorb them. Advertising attempts to make us dissatisfied with our lives so we will buy something to ease our discontent and fill the newly identified need. I like to call it "the call of the mall."

This process is an important part of consumerism, and it can fog our spiritual insight. Our culture, parents, husbands, friends, and bosses send the message that we can never measure up unless we do this or that or that we can't win the approval of certain people unless we sing their song (perfectly). These messages distort our perception of reality.

Distractions and deceptions are like thick lenses over our eyes that distort the way we see God, problems, opportunities, emotions, and people. Some of us need just a small adjustment to see clearly, but others of us have more serious problems. Ophthalmologists treat a wide variety of ocular disorders. I remember when Tim's mother lost her eyesight to diabetes. It caused bleeding in her eyes—she told me it was like looking through muddy water.

I'm certainly not a trained specialist, but I have friends who have suffered from problems such as glaucoma, cataracts, retinal disorders, and conjunctivitis. If a friend or family member suffered from one of these disorders, we'd certainly expect her to see a doctor and get the help she needs. In fact, we'd be shocked if she didn't take steps to regain good vision. It's so important to her health and happiness, we'd wonder about her sanity if she neglected to pursue treatment. But in the spiritual world, many of us are content to live with clouded vision of our emotions, which causes us to wander in confusion and not enjoy our closest relationships as much as we should. We settle for just getting through the day instead of really enjoying all God has for us.

As Jesus said, if we don't have spiritual perception, our whole lives will be full of darkness. What does that darkness look like? Despair, rage, seductive desires, envy, hopelessness, and exhaustion. Basically the opposite of the fruit of the Spirit.

John wrote in his Gospel, "Light has come into the world, but men [and women] loved darkness instead of light" (John 3:19). That indictment is true of lost people, and even those who believe in Christ sometimes feel more comfortable hiding in darkness instead of facing the light of truth. It's human nature. Exposure is scary, and it threatens us to the core. Some of the most courageous women I know are those who have been willing to take a hard look in the mirror and face the facts of their lives. Some of those facts are grand and glorious, but some are bitter pills to swallow. It would be easier to say, "Those things don't bother me," or "They aren't true at all," or "It's somebody else's fault, not mine." Jesus, however, always invited people to be completely honest. They somehow understood that he didn't condemn them but rather loved them and offered forgiveness, restoration, and healing.

Answering piercing questions about our perceptions can eventually lead to more freedom, joy, and love than we ever imagined. For instance, do we see God as he really is, or have we painted a picture of him that is pleasant but distant, uncaring, weak, unthreatening, and inaccurate? When we look in the Scriptures, we find in Christ a blend of traits we find in no other person in history. He is supremely powerful, creating the vast expanse of the universe with a word, but he is as tender as a mother gently caring for her children.

In The Chronicles of Narnia, C.S. Lewis depicts Aslan, the noble lion who is the Christ-figure in the stories, as both kind and terrifying. Often, he appears just in the nick of time when the children are in trouble, but at other times, he vanishes without a trace. Behind every moment of the story, however, he always knows what's happening, and he is working his grand and mysterious purposes.

The Bible tells us that in addition to being strong and kind, God is with you every moment of every day. Do your clouded perceptions leave you feeling alone? When you feel isolated and abandoned, it's easy to cower in fear or lash out in anger. But when the eyes of our hearts tell us that God is Emmanuel, God with us, we feel safe and secure, comforted and loved. Therefore, we are accountable to God to make good choices, to trust in his goodness and strength even in the toughest moments, to think, and to do the right things.

How would you live if you were completely convinced that God is with you at every moment? Picture what your life would look like. You would probably cut down on the gossiping. No wilting in fear, exploding in anger, or being overwhelmed by sorrow. In his presence, you would no doubt bask far more in his love, trust more fully in his strength, and more wholeheartedly follow his wise leading wherever he might take you. You would embrace his grace for your damaged emotions.

Eyes of faith help us find our way to the feet of Jesus to enjoy his love and listen to him teach us. Like the men and women who followed him, we quickly realize that his view of priorities is quite the opposite of the way the world looks at things. He taught that the way to achieve greatness is to be the servant of all. The way up is down, the inside is more important than the outside, and "the least of these" are God's highest priority.

I'm sure people often walked away from Jesus scratching their heads. A recurring theme in his teaching was that the true fulfillment we all desire comes not from filling our lives with possessions, positions, and popularity, but from selflessly devoting ourselves to him and his cause. He told those who followed him, "If anyone would come after me, he must deny himself and take up his cross and follow me. For whoever wants to save his life will lose it, but whoever loses his life for me will find it" (Matthew 16:24-25).

Eyes of faith enable us to treasure what God treasures and follow his ways even when people around us are going in a different direction. Only those with spiritual perception are willing to lose their lives in order to find true meaning and joy. Instead of reacting to disappointments by complaining, we can tenaciously look for God's hand at work behind the scenes and cultivate an attitude of thankfulness. Instead of caving in to others' demands so we can avoid the pain of conflict, we can speak up with courage and diplomacy. Instead of choosing the easy and enticing path to gossip about a friend, we can hold our tongues and suggest prayer as a better option. Eyes of faith don't often lead us down the easiest path, but they identify the way that pleases God, and in him, we find true joy and peace.

Trusting God with Tomorrow Gives Meaning to Today

The God-given ability to see beyond our emotions certainly applies to the situations and people we face each day, but spiritual perception also allows us to see far into the future. It's like talking with my kids about situations they face while growing up. Sometimes doing what's right doesn't always *feel* right in the moment, but in the end you know you made the right decision. This can be tough to do and requires spiritual perspective, spiritual power, and a spiritual stability that your decision or action is right.

Someday, the transformation of the universe that began with the resurrection of Jesus will permeate every atom in all creation. The Scriptures tell us that God won't do away with the world as we know it; he'll use it to create a new heaven and new earth. Our certainty of the future gives us courage for today. Author and bishop N.T. Wright has written extensively that the resurrection of Jesus points to a glorious future reality, a reality that inspires hope today and powerfully motivates us to live for Christ each day. In his book *Following Jesus*, he connects these concepts:

> Every act of justice, every word of truth, every creation of genuine beauty, every act of sacrificial love, will be reaffirmed on the last day, in the new world. The poem that glimpses truth in a new way, the mug of tea given with gentleness to the down-and-out at the drop-in center; the setting aside of my own longings in order to support and cherish someone who depends on me; the piece of work done honestly and thoroughly; the prayer that comes from heart and mind together; all of these and many more are building blocks for the kingdom. We may not yet see how they will fit into God's eventual structure, but the fact of the resurrection, of God's glad reaffirmation of true humanness, assures us that they will.[3]

As we'll see in every chapter of this book, spiritual perception helps us understand our powerful emotions and gives us hope for today and tomorrow.

Thankfully, God is supremely patient with us. Even those who followed Jesus most closely didn't grasp the depth of his insights. Sometimes, their painful emotions threatened to overwhelm them. I love the moment just after the disciples wakened Jesus in the middle of a fierce storm because their boat was sinking. They were terrified! With no apparent fanfare, Jesus woke up and calmed the wind and waves. No problem there. The disciples looked at each other and asked, "Who is this guy?" They had thought they understood who he was, but regardless of how much they grasped, he was more wondrous still.

Wonder is an important element in spiritual sight. If we're not amazed with Jesus, fascinated by his wisdom, and awestruck by his power, we don't know who he really is. Solomon told us, "The fear [reverential awe] of the LORD is the beginning of knowledge." Spiritual perception begins with an increasing understanding of the awesome greatness and profound goodness of God. He is the source of light, and in the beacon of his truth we learn to see every person, circumstance, problem, and opportunity with the eyesight of faith. And the great news is that he loves you and me.

When our lives are filled with love, peace, and hope, the expression in our eyes changes. The lines around the edges soften. Angry glares and fearful glances are transformed into looks of confidence and joy. (And we may not need as much shadow and mascara to hide our expressions.) *changes*

My Hope for You

If you've looked at the table of contents, you know where we're going. We'll look at a wide range of damaged emotions. Some of us are hiding (more or less effectively) unresolved hurts, shattering fears, deep anger, and unthinkable desires. We'll look at some women in the Bible who faced similar challenges, and we'll uncover principles to help us face these difficulties with understanding and hope.

I wish that with the press of a button, all of us would receive crystal-clear perception, but gaining clearer spiritual perception isn't like LASIK surgery, which promises instant and complete cures! No, gaining spiritual insight is a process, far more of a hike up a beautiful but steep mountain trail than an instant solution. Clear vision doesn't solve all our problems and make all our painful feelings go away, but with accurate perception we can grasp God's design more fully and experience his peace even when we don't have any idea what he's up to.

You may be reading this book to gain insights for yourself, or you may be reading it to help someone you love. Either way, I trust God will answer for you the prayer Paul prayed for the Christians in Ephesus many years ago:

> I keep asking that the God of our Lord Jesus Christ, the glorious Father, may give you the Spirit of wisdom and revelation, so that you may know him better. I pray also that the eyes of your heart may be enlightened in order that you may know the hope to which he has called you, the riches of his glorious inheritance in the saints, and his incomparably great power for us who believe (Ephesians 1:17-19).

I hope God gives you courage to be honest as you look in the mirror. Your eyes are windows to your soul. When you look, I hope you see lots of joy, peace, and love. But regardless of what you see in your reflection, you can be assured that God offers his grace to you and wants to give you richer, deeper, clearer spiritual sight than you've ever known before. With his love and insight, even the most damaged emotions can be healed. It takes time and courage. You wouldn't have picked up this book if you weren't ready to take God's hand and take steps forward, so let's do.

At the end of each chapter, you'll find some reflection questions. When I read books, I get far more out of them if I take a little time to consider the issues the author presents. These questions will help you gain insights about your reflections and perceptions. I hope you enjoy working through them. And by the way, they stimulate rich discussions with your husband, friends, class, or small group.

Healing the Damage

1. Do you know anyone who can "read" people by looking at the expression in their eyes? How does this gift help her in her relationships?

2. In what sense are there no good or bad emotions?

3. How can God use even our most painful emotions in positive ways in our lives?

4. Read Matthew 6:22-23. In what ways is your eye a lamp, and what does it mean for your body to be full of light?

5. How does perceiving God as wonderful affect every aspect your life? How does perceiving him as disinterested and powerless affect you?

6. Reflect quietly and deeply on Jesus' statement in Matthew 16:24-25. What emotions do these verses stimulate? Tell why.

7. What do you hope to get out of this book?

8. Read Ephesians 1:17-19. Paraphrase Paul's words and make this prayer your own as you begin reading this book.

1

Anxious and Afraid

Many of us crucify ourselves between two thieves—
regret for the past and fear of the future.

FULTON OURSLER

Tim was out of town. Zach was with a friend. It was the perfect weekend for Megan and me to begin spring cleaning.

After a few hours of dusting, sweeping, and washing the windows, we decided to go shopping for hanging baskets and planters to put on the porch and by our pool. Trying to figure out what flowers, plants, and colors would look best, we visited a variety of places. Before long, as often seems to happen, we were back at the very first landscaping company we had visited. The beautiful planters and hanging baskets there were in full bloom and lined up in neat rows on piles of wood chips. We carefully chose the nicest ones we could find and paid the clerk, who loaded them in our car.

Little did we know what else we had in the car as we headed home.

I pulled through our circular driveway and parked near the front door to our house. Megan and I jumped out and began unloading the planters and sitting them right inside the door.

"Mom," said Megan, "I think that's all of them. Do you want me to take the hanging baskets down by the pool?"

"Yes, if you would please, that would be great," I said as I finished unloading the other items we had bought on our trip. As I was closing the hatch, I heard one of the most bloodcurdling screams I've ever heard.

"Aaahhh!" screamed Megan, "There's a snake in the house!"

I immediately ran up the front steps, and sure enough, in the corner of the room was a snake.

Picture Megan and me standing in the house, looking a snake square in the face and wondering what to do. It must have been in one of the planters, which means it was with us in the car and one of us carried it into our house!

You think snakes are bad? You should see Tim when he comes across a spider. It's a scene that would put any *Saturday Night Live* skit to shame. To see him dance around the living room is priceless.

As a counselor, though, he understands fear well. One time he was standing under a tree and a snake actually fell on him! To this day he insists that every time he sees a snake he can feel it wrapping around his neck. It's a good thing he was out of town the day the snake came home with Megan and me.

Fear of spiders or snakes is common, but Tim says that people aren't sure whether those fears are innate. Some psychologists suggest that we are born with five fears; others say we are born with two. People are most commonly afraid of these five things:

> death
>
> embarrassment
>
> love lost
>
> rejection
>
> heights (falling)

A recent Gallup poll asked teenagers ages 13 to 15 what their greatest fear was. Here are the top ten responses, starting with the most common:

> terrorist attacks
>
> spiders

death

failure

war

heights

criminal or gang violence

being alone

the future

nuclear war[1]

Are you afraid of any of these? I know I am—especially now that we know we're no longer impervious to things like terrorist attacks and violence. While I was writing this book, John Allen Muhammad, most commonly known as the DC sniper, was executed in Virginia seven years after he and his accomplice, Lee Boyd Malvo, murdered ten people around that area. His execution reawakened many DC area residents' fears and prompted them to once again reevaluate their daily routines to avoid becoming the next victim.[2]

Fear is the natural response to a real or perceived threat of imminent danger, evil, or pain. It's always a response to something in the future, something that is going to happen or that we think is going to happen. Take a moment and consider this: What are some of your own greatest fears? How do you react when you face something that you are afraid of?

Fear in Relationships

Two sisters showcase the different ways fear can control people's lives. They were just a few years apart, they grew up together, and they were now in their thirties. That's where the similarities end. When I met Suzanne, I was immediately impressed by her sunny disposition. She always had a kind word for those who crossed her path each day. The first time I saw her encounter a difficulty, I noticed that she instantly stated her steadfast trust in God. As time went on and others around her faced various kinds of heartache, she unflinchingly wore a smile and spoke words of faith.

I appreciate people who trust God through thick and thin, but Suzanne was different. She seemed incapable of realistically facing the hard facts of life. When I heard about Suzanne's child's debilitating, life-threatening sickness, I expressed sadness and hugged her, but Suzanne again reported cheerily, "Oh, don't worry. God is in control, and we can trust him." I suspected that Suzanne's superficial spirituality was covering up something very painful, but I had no idea what it was.

Then I met her sister. Brittany certainly looked like Suzanne— similar facial features, hair texture and color, and other physical attributes—but her demeanor and Suzanne's were as opposite as day and night. Brittany was tough, hard-nosed, willing to "call it like she saw it," never sugarcoating any painful event or awkward relationship. She was in control of every moment of her life, demanding agreement and instant compliance from those who reported to her.

For a few days I was with both women, and I was amazed at the contrast in their outlook, attitude, and behavior. They were raised in the same home, but they seemed to be from two different planets! I hadn't gotten very far in trying to break through Suzanne's protective shell, so I took a chance to talk to Brittany. Completely in character, she told the unvarnished truth.

"Our family was really screwed up," she said without a hint of self-consciousness or self-pity. "Dad was a drunk, and he beat Mom, Suzanne, and me when he came home after his binges. He always apologized later, but the damage was done."

I asked, "How do you think his abuse affected you?"

Brittany glared at me with steely resolution. "I decided no one would ever hurt me again—*never*." And she meant it. As it turns out, Brittany's and Suzanne's relationships are poisoned with the fear that someone is going to hurt them.

Fear is likely the most common human emotion. I'd like to say it's love, joy, or peace, but I don't think that's the case. In fact, fear is so common that we don't even recognize it. We're like fish who don't realize we're wet. Our responses to fear vary: Some of us are paralyzed, and others of us are compelled to control our surroundings. But all of us experience fear to some degree, and unless we respond to it honestly and courageously, it will probably shape our lives in unhealthy ways.

What are women afraid of? Almost anything. One of the biggies is rejection. We long to be connected, to feel loved and safe, and we're afraid that the people we value won't treasure us. We may be afraid of failure—at work, at church, at home, or in bed—hoping we can succeed enough to meet someone's standard and become acceptable. We may be afraid of being penniless, so we hoard our money. Or conversely, we may be afraid of being excluded from a certain group unless we keep up appearances, so we spend too much money on clothes, cars, and the spa.

Fears create their own treadmills because acceptance and success are so fleeting. Even when we get the approval and acclaim we long for, the good feelings don't last long. Then we realize we have to do even more to stay in the spotlight, and we feel even more driven to perform.

We naturally assess the risks in any venture or personal encounter, and we determine whether the potential gain is worth the gamble. Many women feel caught in the no-man's-land between hope and fear, especially in relationships with men. Canadian journalist and author Merle Shain observed, "Loving can cost a lot, but not loving always costs more, and those who fear to love often find that want of love is an emptiness that robs the joy from life."[3] When we shrink back in fear, we think we're protecting ourselves from harm, but often we are actually preventing ourselves from experiencing real life. Certainly, we don't want to take foolish risks and trust untrustworthy people, but we can learn to trust wisely and cautiously.

Alone at the Well

In the first century AD, most Jews who traveled from Judea to Galilee took a circuitous route around Samaria. Jews detested Samaritans because they were half-breeds, religious apostates, and former political enemies. Good Jews wouldn't even talk to Samaritans, much less develop relationships with them. But of course, Jesus was not like most first-century Jews. I'm sure Jesus' disciples were perplexed when he chose to lead them straight through Samaria.

At noon near the town of Sychar, Jesus sat by a well while his disciples went into town to buy food. As Jesus waited for them to return, a woman came to draw water from the well. All the other women from the city had come early in the morning at the customary time, but she came at noon. Why? Was she trying to avoid them?

She was an adulteress, an outcast among outcasts. She probably avoided other women because she was tired of their sneers and cat-calls. Did her fear determine her daily schedule and keep her isolated? Probably, but Jesus saw beneath her fear and spoke to her heart.

From his clothing, she would have recognized he was a Jew and assumed he was prejudiced against her. When Jesus opened the dialogue by asking her to give him a drink of water, she was undoubtedly shocked. As the conversation progressed, Jesus spoke truthfully but graciously. He drew her relational secrets out of the shadows and into the light, but instead of condemning her, his demeanor and initiative assured her of his love and forgiveness. When he revealed that he was the Messiah, the one she had been looking for, her fears melted in his love, and she believed. She was so excited about this seemingly chance and amazingly freeing encounter with the Messiah that she ran into town to tell everyone she knew—even those who had rejected her—about the forgiveness and love she had found.

When the disciples came back and saw what was happening, they were likely shaking their heads and thinking, *Now what's he doing? We go to town for a cheeseburger, and he skips lunch to hang out with her!* The apostle John later wrote, "There is no fear in love.

But perfect love drives out fear, because fear has to do with punishment" (1 John 4:18). She had lived her life under a cloud of fear— fear of rejection, fear of abandonment, fear of ridicule—but Jesus' love pierced all of her heart's defenses and doubts. She became a new woman.

> I am not afraid of tomorrow, for I have
> seen yesterday and I love today.
> WILLIAM ALLEN WHITE

Just for fun, here are a few uncommon fears.

anthrophobia: fear of flowers

arithmophobia: fear of numbers

bibliophobia: fear of books

clinophobia: fear of beds

paedophobia: fear of children

hypnophobia: fear of sleep and falling asleep

lyssophobia: fear of insanity

phobatrivaphobia: fear of trivia about phobias

dromophobia: fear of crossing the road

unatractiphobia: fear of ugly people

arachibutyrophobia: fear of peanut butter sticking to the roof
    of the mouth

cathisophobia: fear of sitting

hippopotomonstrosesquippedaliophobia: fear of long words

scolionophobia: fear of school

urophobia: fear of urine or urinating

xenoglossophobia: fear of foreign languages

A few weeks ago I was driving along Route 501, a four-lane highway that I take often on my way home. Minding my own business and cruising along at the speed limit, I came up on another car moving fairly slowly, but I was afraid to pass it. The car was weaving back and forth from lane to lane, sometimes just straddling the centerline. I didn't know whether the driver was drunk, asleep, or just not paying attention. After I had followed the car for about a mile, I finally mustered up the courage to go around it. As I did, I saw the driver—a college-age girl texting on her cell phone. Just another reason to be afraid of driving.

Some fears are clearly helpful! Speeding along a crowded highway next to a driver who is texting on her phone produces a legitimate fear and calls for an intelligent response, like quickly passing her, or slowing down and following her, or maybe throwing a purse at her! (We will deal with that later.) When people in California feel the earth move, they experience very normal and reasonable fear for their safety. Healthy fears of danger keep us alert and responsive. We do well to pay attention to them and act accordingly—unless they grow inordinately and consume our lives.

But what about the devastating, consuming fears, the ones that make us feel out of control because they have taken over our lives? They threaten our stability and security, so we lash out in anger or cower in terror. We scramble to establish some sense of stability and carve out some measure of meaning in our lives. Our fears make us feel terribly vulnerable, so we attack at the slightest provocation, or we hide from even the faintest hint of trouble. We build high, thick walls to protect our hearts, but those walls prevent us from getting close to anyone. We lie in order to make ourselves look a little better than others or to make them look a little worse than us. Sooner or later, we may have told so many lies that we don't even remember what's true anymore.

When fears control our lives, we feel like victims, and soon, we can't see ourselves in any other way. We believe we've been wronged by people and by God, and we demand that somebody make us feel better. Self-pity eventually leads to passivity. Instead of taking action to change the situation, we wait for someone to do it for us—but they seldom do. We become fragile and demanding, easily hurt but expecting others to jump through our hoops. When they don't, we're hurt yet again, and the cycle continues.

Those whose lives are shaped by fear engage in black-and-white thinking. They don't feel safe and secure enough to see shades of gray and make hard choices, so they automatically try to simplify their world by seeing people as either all good or all bad. They are either all the way in relationships or all the way out of them. Oftentimes this is because the people they were supposed to love or trust were the very people who hurt them, making relationships a bewildering mix of joy and pain.

I remember meeting with a woman who swore up and down that her husband was cheating on her. They tremendously enjoyed their times together when he was home, but whenever he left town on business, she called his cell phone every 30 minutes to be sure he was where he said he would be. If he didn't answer or call her back, she called his hotel. Every time he returned home, she gave him the silent treatment until he apologized for not picking up his phone. Once he had been home long enough for her to feel safe again, they were back to loving each other like newlyweds. But her fear that he was cheating paralyzed her and stifled their marriage. As a result, her worst fears eventually came to pass—not because he cheated, but because she was out of control. He'd had it.

Extreme fears become diagnosable phobias and consume people's lives, robbing them of joy and freedom. Fear is a central component in obsessive-compulsive behavior, panic attacks, and other types of fear-related disorders in which people feel compelled to control themselves or their environment in an attempt to feel safe.

Some relationships or situations are truly threatening. In these situations, fear is completely reasonable, and we need to take steps to protect ourselves. If we find ourselves in relationships like these, rational fear should drive us to take action: to speak truth, set boundaries, avoid trusting untrustworthy people, and offer steps forward toward a healthier relationship based on trust and respect. If the person agrees, the relationship can be restored. It is foolish, though, to trust people who have proven to be untrustworthy. Overcoming our fears doesn't make us vulnerable to abusive people; rather, it empowers us to muster our courage and take steps of faith to protect ourselves and offer a path of reconciliation.

> You gain strength, courage, and confidence by every
> experience in which you really stop to look fear in the face.
> You must do the thing which you think you cannot do.
> ELEANOR ROOSEVELT

Steps Forward

If you want to change a situation, the first step is to accurately assess it. Many women remain mired in fear because they don't even realize they are afraid. When one lady studied this subject and reflected on her life, she told me sadly, "Julie, I've never realized until today that my entire life has been under a cloud of fear. Everything I've done, everything I've said, and every relationship I've had has been shaped by my fear of being alone. What in the world can I do about it?" She had already taken the first step toward hope and healing.

God is well aware of how fragile we are and how fear can consume our hearts and paralyze us. Many women I know are afraid of failure. Others fear rejection. I don't believe it's a coincidence that the command "Do not fear" is found 365 times in the Bible. We need to hear it every day. Don't be surprised when the Holy Spirit taps you on the shoulder and whispers, *You're acting out of fear. Remember I'm with you and be courageous.*

We may think that fear and faith are completely separate and never occupy the same space in our hearts, but that's not true. Faith isn't the absence of fear, but the choice to depend on God's truth and power even when we're afraid. I can sense the comfort and courage the psalmist must have felt when he wrote, "When I am afraid, I will trust in you" (Psalm 56:3). He didn't write that he would trust God after his fears were gone or when he wasn't afraid at all. No, in the middle of his fear, he chose to trust in God's goodness, strength, and wisdom.

Fears that are deeply rooted in a painful past don't magically disappear. They gradually took up residence in our lives, and God's grace can gradually dissolve them. This process includes other people, for just as we are wounded in relationships, we experience healing and hope in relationships. Find a trusted friend to talk with—someone who doesn't have instant answers for long-term problems, someone who understands and has compassion for you, someone who points you back to Christ's perfect love, which casts out our inordinate fears. That's the key: Experience God's love and strength more deeply every day, and let his goodness and greatness fill your heart and replace your fears.

Your trusted friend will help you face your fears and develop new skills to handle life. Instead of shrinking back in hopeless passivity, you'll learn to speak up, chart a new course, and take action toward your goals. You won't demand compliance from people because love will replace your fear, and you'll be able to truly care for people instead of controlling them.

Many women keep acting and feeling the same way day after day and year after year because they simply don't believe there's any other way to live. I'm here to tell you there *is* another way to live! We have a choice! We don't have to be driven by our fears. We can admit they exist, talk to wise friends who help us process our buried pain, change our perceptions of reality, and take bold steps to get our lives back. When we do, the whole world opens up to us.

When you are honest with yourself, do you see any areas of your life that show the effects of inordinate, controlling fear? Do you have a friend or family member who needs someone like you to help her take steps toward melting those fears in the love of God? Take a moment to consider whether today could be the day that you begin to face your fears in a new way.

Healing the Damage

1. What are some of the most common fears women experience?

2. How do these fears control their lives, make them feel fragile, and compel them to protect themselves?

3. What are some completely helpful fears? When do they become unhelpful?

4. Read John 4:1-42. How did the Samaritan woman demonstrate her fears? How did Jesus speak to her heart? How did she respond?

5. How do fears often lead to self-pity and passivity?

6. Do any inordinate fears control your life? Explain your answer.

7. If they do, who is a trusted friend you can talk to?

Bible Passages on Fear

"There is no fear in love. But perfect love drives out fear, because fear has to do with punishment. The one who fears is not made perfect in love" (1 John 4:18).

"Even though I walk
    through the valley of the shadow of death,

I will fear no evil,
> for you are with me;
your rod and your staff,
> they comfort me" (Psalm 23:4).

"The LORD is my light and my salvation
> whom shall I fear?
The LORD is the stronghold of my life
> of whom shall I be afraid?" (Psalm 27:1).

"The LORD is for me; I will not be afraid.
> What can man do to me?" (Psalm 118:6).

"For God has not given us a spirit of fear and timidity, but of power, love, and self-discipline" (2 Timothy 1:7 NLT).

"But the love of the LORD remains forever
> with those who fear him.
His salvation extends to the children's children"
> (Psalm 103:17 NLT).

"All you who fear the LORD, trust the LORD!
> He is your helper and your shield"
> (Psalm 115:11 NLT).

"Praise the LORD.
Blessed is the man who fears the LORD,
> who finds great delight in his commands"
> (Psalm 112:1).

"Though a mighty army surrounds me,
> my heart will not be afraid.
Even if I am attacked,
> I will remain confident" (Psalm 27:3 NLT).

Hurt: How Pain Steals Our Joy

*If we will be quiet and ready enough, we shall
find compensation in every disappointment.*

HENRY DAVID THOREAU

As I double-checked my list, I felt great.

Do the dishes—check.

Clean the house—check.

Wash and fold the clothes—check.

Pay the bills—check.

Go by the bank—check.

Take Simba to the vet for shots—check.

I'd had a productive day indeed…until Tim came home.

"Hey, honey," he yelled as he walked through the door.

"Hi!" I shouted back happily. As Tim made his way down the stairs to greet me, he immediately noticed two things. First, I was in my sweats getting ready to work out. Second, a pile of clean and folded clothes was lying on the pool table, ready to be put away.

"What did you do today?" he muttered. "Did you get a chance to get out?"

Clearly, he thought I didn't do anything but lie around in my sweats. You can imagine what was going through my mind. *He thinks I sat at home all day and did nothing!* I was having a PMS (pretty mean sister) day to top it off, and for a moment I considered knocking him out. Just wait until the next time he shows up to a baseball game and Zach's uniform isn't washed. Just wait until he has to do his own laundry, take his own dog to the vet, help Zach with school projects, and make sure the mortgage is paid. Didn't he know that I taped two phone interviews and that I was leaving for a conference on Thursday? And somebody has to buy the groceries!

Don't get me wrong, Tim is awesome and appreciates me and the things I do for him and our children. But every now and then, I can feel a little underappreciated, and that hurts.

Step back and look at your life. The pace today is much faster than ever. And though we've been promised that technology will give us more free time, the opposite has proven true. It gives us more connectivity, so we try to cram in more content. We live at a frantic pace, spending less time in reflection, leisure, and relationships. We expect to get more done in less time, and we rush from one thing to another, trying to turn a busy life into a full one. Yet when the day is over, we lie in bed exhausted, overwhelmed, pressured, and underappreciated, wondering when we'll see the abundant life, the "life to the full" that Jesus promised (John 10:10).

The pace and pressure of today's world intensifies the pain and tears we have built up through the years. Hurt accumulates through violence and abuse and also through repeated negative, condemning messages from people who supposedly loved you and who you thought were trustworthy. Painful experiences like these function like sandpaper on a woman's soul, wearing away her confidence, stability, happiness, hope, and joy.

> History, despite its wrenching pain, cannot be unlived,
> but if faced with courage, need not be lived again.
> MAYA ANGELOU

The Wounded Heart

Abuse, domestic violence, miscarriages, pain-filled marriages, single parenting with no money, caring for aging parents...These are a few of the many unique challenges in a woman's world, and the list continues. An empty nest, PMS, menopause, finances, breast cancer...The list goes on and on. Most studies indicate that at least 33 percent of American women have been beaten, forced into sex, or otherwise abused. A quarter of the women in North America were molested in childhood.[1]

According to the Guttmacher Institute, 35 percent of American women will have had an abortion by the time they reach 45.[2] Usually left open and unhealed, such hurts add turmoil and stress to a woman's everyday life and her closest relationships. As a result, it's easy to get angry, to feel cheated, to want to stay in bed. No wonder women are approximately twice as likely as men to suffer from major depression and dysthymia. Depression has been called the most significant mental health risk for women, especially younger women of childbearing and childrearing age.[3] The lifetime risk of developing irritable bowel syndrome is about 30 percent, and 5 to 10 percent of women and girls suffer from an eating disorder.[4]

Every day I come across single women who are struggling to find life partners. I meet married women who are frustrated with theirs and living with unfulfilled longing. Our culture adds further strain by devaluing women or by promoting a controlling, dominating radical feminism.

When we're wounded, we focus on protecting ourselves. We hide our true feelings (even from ourselves), and we carve out a lifestyle that offers some type of safety. Some of us are so desperate for love that we live to please people so they'll say, "I really appreciate you." But in our compulsion to please, we often smother people with attention, and sooner or later, they distance themselves from us.

Others of us have determined that the way to find safety and significance is to win at all costs. These deeply wounded women compensate for their pain by becoming domineering and command-ing authority. They have to be in charge of every person and every situation, and they deeply resent anyone who questions them.

Women who are deeply hurt naturally compensate by hiding behind a smile, pleasing people to win acceptance, and proving themselves by dominating their competition. But they live every day with a hard shell around their hearts. The love they long for remains just out of reach. They've come to the sad conclusion that this pattern of coping with heartache is the best they can hope for, so they spend their time trying new techniques of hiding their true feelings, dancing to other's demands to win approval, and demand-ing compliance from those around them.

Noted psychologist Ernest Becker wrote not long ago that "mod-ern man is drinking and drugging himself out of awareness, or he spends his time shopping, which is the same thing."[5] When we're wounded, we reach for anything to fill the emptiness in our souls and the holes in our hearts. But we often go beyond pleasing others and try to prove ourselves. Alcohol, drugs, shopping, food, sex, per-fectionism, fantasy and romance novels, obsession with makeovers and external beauty, and emotional affairs are some of the things we use to numb our pain. They may or may not work for a short time, but they can never provide real, eternal life (see 2 Corinthians 4:18). Empty, exhausted, and yearning for something more, we'll reach for anything to calm, soothe, and fulfill the longings deep inside us that are screaming to be met.

This false way of escape keeps us from the spiritual fresh air we need. Dallas Willard alluded to this when he wrote, "Obviously, the problem is a spiritual one. And so must be the cure."[6]

I have come to realize that the more I continue to look to Tim, to my children, or to the world to feel appreciated and affirmed for everything I do, the more I'll be left feeling that what I do is never enough. When we look to other things and people to fill the holes in our souls, we turn away from God and eventually lose a sense of who we were created to be.

All of us face disappointments. Some are devastating. But with an abiding sense of hope, we can see God's hand at work or trust him when we can't. On the other hand, if we don't invite God into our wounds and disappointments, we will collapse into despair.

Naomi's Despair

Whenever I think I've got it bad, I just need to reread the first chapter of the book of Ruth. In the ancient Near East, women trusted men to protect them and provide for them. Women had no social safety net other than the men in their lives. In fact, women's identity was based on their marriages and their ability to have sons. With that in mind, the conversation between Naomi and her daughters-in-law is even more poignant.

Circumstances conspired against Naomi. A famine in Bethlehem had forced her family to flee to the land of Moab, where she lived with her husband, Elimelech, her two sons, Mahlon and Kilion, and their Moabite wives, Orpah and Ruth. The writer doesn't tell us what happened, but in that foreign land, Elimelech died, and a few years after his death, Naomi's beloved sons also died.

Relocation to a foreign country and the death of your husband and your two sons—that's enough to devastate anyone. Most of us could fall back on some kind of support system and maintain at least a semblance of an independent identity. In Naomi's world, however, every shred of stability and happiness was ripped from her. Even though she had two daughters-in-law, she felt completely alone. She decided to return home to Bethlehem, and she sent Ruth and Orpah back to their homes in Moab. They wept and insisted that they go with her, but Naomi stubbornly refused.

> Go back, my dear daughters. Why would you come with me? Do you suppose I still have sons in my womb who can become your future husbands? Go back, dear daughters—on your way, please! I'm too old to get a husband. Why, even if I said, "There's still hope!" and this very night got a man and had sons, can you imagine being satisfied to

wait until they were grown? Would you wait that long to get married again? No, dear daughters; this is a bitter pill for me to swallow—more bitter for me than for you. God has dealt me a hard blow (Ruth 1:11-13 MSG).

As Naomi continued sending the young women away, we get a glimpse into her heart. Her perceptions of God, of life, and of herself were clouded by doubt and disappointment.

You may know the rest of the story. Orpah left for home, but Ruth was steadfastly devoted to her gloomy mother-in-law. Did Ruth's love change Naomi's heart? Not immediately. When they walked into Bethlehem, Naomi greeted old friends dismally.

Don't call me Naomi; call me Bitter. The Strong One has dealt me a bitter blow. I left here full of life, and God has brought me back with nothing but the clothes on my back. Why would you call me Naomi? God certainly doesn't. The Strong One ruined me (Ruth 1:20-21 MSG).

Nothing, it seemed, could raise her spirits and clear her vision to see the amazing hope God had for her.

> I have learned now that while those who
> speak about one's miseries usually hurt,
> those who keep silence hurt more.
>
> C.S. LEWIS

Fresh Insights

Abuse, violence, culture...all of these lie. We even lie to ourselves.

When we're pounded by a troubled past or a perpetually pain-filled life and reaching toward heaven brings about little or slow change, we might wonder, *Can God make a difference? Does he care about my situation? Does he even exist?*

"I don't want to be entertained anymore; I need answers and clear direction. Help from God would be good. Where is he when I need him? Why doesn't he help me?" This is what one woman said to me recently.

Lies can wreck marriages, families, and careers. Struggling with an addiction can stifle the heart's cry. Many women can relate to David's cry in Psalm 6:6: "I am worn out from groaning; all night long I flood my bed with weeping and drench my couch with tears."

God created us as emotional beings with an innate (and quite marvelous) capacity to feel a whole range of emotions—good, bad, and ugly. Think about it with me for a moment. Picture your last good cry. You may be thinking of a time you cried because you were hurting, but you could just as easily be recalling a time when you cried because of uncontrollable laughter.

The ability to *feel* is one of God's greatest gifts to us, but when it is out of sync, it can lead to low self-worth and spiritual purposelessness. Instead of living in the freedom of healthy emotions, we can become emotional wrecks. However, emotional wreckage breaks a woman down. It handicaps her from being able to function. This is not the way God designed us to live!

The lies that we sometimes believe—that we are too needy, too emotional, or too strong-willed, or that we are not pretty enough, efficient enough, or kind enough—flow from hearts that are filled with shame, deceit, and guilt.

Paul writes in his letter to the Galatians, "It is for freedom that Christ has set us free. Stand firm, then, and do not let yourselves be burdened again by a yoke of slavery" (Galatians 5:1).

One of the reasons Christ came to set us free is so our hearts can and will be satisfied in him and conformed to his image. To carry out his plan, he uses life's difficulties to reveal our needs, weaknesses, and sin.

Mary Magdalene was bound by the yoke of slavery until Jesus drove seven demons out of her. The number seven refers to perfection, so Mary seems to have represented ultimate slavery to evil. Surely people secretly talked about her behind her back. She was defined by her imprisonment.

Luke honors Mary by naming her first among the women who traveled with the disciples. But he refers to her as "Mary, from whom seven demons had gone out." Why would that terrible tagline stay with her? Perhaps her slavery and bondage to evil is a great representation of the power of the freedom of Christ through his death on the cross. The new life and light that guides her stands in stark contrast to the dark and miserable life she once lived.

God encouraged the Israelites to remember their slavery in Egypt (Deuteronomy 7:7-8). Paul reminded the Corinthians of their humble beginnings (1 Corinthians 1:26-31) and pointed out that the Ephesians were once "without hope and without God in the world" (Ephesians 2:12). The principle of Scripture is to remember our former slavery so we can remember the one who has set us free.

Living with joy and freedom in our hearts means we don't dwell on the past. Instead, we remember the great Redeemer and Restorer who set our hearts free from the past, and we embrace the freedom that Christ has provided for us in his suffering. Gradually, we begin to understand why God tells us to rejoice in our sufferings and why Paul boasted in his weakness. Those things highlight God's powerful work in us.

But getting free from the past doesn't mean we pretend it never happened. We won't make any progress if we deny the reality of an abusive relationship, minimize our disappointments, overlook our stress, or excuse others who caused our hurt. Facing the facts is the first step in healing. I'm comforted when I remember that Jesus, the resurrection and the life, was so touched by the death of his friend Lazarus that he wept at his tomb. Jesus knew he was going to raise Lazarus from death to life in only a few minutes, but that didn't minimize the hurt Jesus felt and acknowledged at that moment.

Some people become numb when they despair, but others go

in the opposite direction, analyzing every word, every gesture, and every event that relates to their pain, trying to find answers for their hurt. Analysis is an important part of the healing process, but we should use it to lead us to emotional honesty, grief, and spiritual insights. If we live only in our heads and ignore our hearts, we will miss the true healing God wants to work deep in us.

Sometimes when we hurt, we instantly know why. We may have made a dumb mistake, or we may have willfully sinned. Other people may have accidentally done something that caused consequences for us, or they may have consciously chosen to hurt us. Or perhaps a natural disaster has uprooted our lives. We may experience spiritual conflict against the forces of darkness, or we may feel the pain of being pruned by God (see John 15) as part of our abiding in him. Sooner or later, all of us who follow Christ will experience heartaches that seem to have no rhyme or reason.

We can analyze a situation until we're blue in the face and yet never find its cause. Job endured the worst problems any of us can imagine, but he couldn't find the reason. His friends tried to help by telling Job that he was suffering as a result of his sin, but he knew that the answer wasn't that simple. Again and again, he asked God for a courtroom trial so he could cross-examine the Almighty. Finally, God showed up, but he turned the tables on Job. Now God wasn't the one on the witness stand; Job was. In his monologue, God never answered Job's questions. Instead, he asked 64 penetrating questions of his own to show Job that God is sovereign over all of creation, the ruler of all, who is omnipresent, omnipotent, and omniscient. God's closing argument had the desired effect on Job, who responded to God with chastened, humble faith: "I know that you can do all things; no plan of yours can be thwarted...Surely I spoke of things I did not understand, things too wonderful for me to know" (Job 42:2-3). Job's renewed spiritual vision enabled him to see God's trustworthy character even when he didn't perceive the reasons for his pain.

Strangely, however, many of us prefer to stay stuck in our pain rather than experience the freedom and joy healing brings. Perhaps we've gotten comfortable with life the way it is and prefer that to the trauma of change. Or perhaps self-pity and bitterness just feel right, and letting go of them is difficult. Or maybe the path ahead seems too long and steep, and we don't think we can make it.

When Jesus saw scores of sick and crippled people by the pool in John 5, he asked one of them a simple question, "Do you want to get well?" I believe he is asking many of us the same question today. Failure to respond to Jesus' gracious invitation leaves us lonely, afraid, and angry. Then, day after day and year after year, the bitter weeds of fear and anger grow in our hearts, and sooner or later, these weeds choke the life out of us. Every cherished relationship sours because we are demanding and defensive, or we become compulsive doers to prove ourselves to others, or we wilt in passivity. The light of hope vanishes from our eyes, and we settle for merely enduring each day.

From time to time, disappointment is a reality in all of our lives, but it need not result in hopeless despair. God wants to use every moment in our lives—the good and the bad—to shape us. Our goal, then, isn't to get rid of our painful past. Our goal is to trust God to use it for good. In his book *The Healing Path*, psychologist Dan Allender describes the spiritual perception we can have about even the most painful events in our lives:

> If we fail to anticipate thoughtfully how we will respond to the harm of living in a fallen world, the pain may be for naught. It will either numb or destroy us rather than refine and even bless us...Healing in this life is not the resolution of our past; it is the use of our past to draw us into deeper relationship with God and His purposes for our lives.[7]

You will know that forgiveness has begun when you recall those who hurt you and feel the power to wish them well.
LOUIS B. SMEDES

Steps Forward

When Naomi was in the depths of despair amid a tangled web of hopeless thoughts, God gave her a treasured friend who wouldn't let go. I love Ruth. All of us need a friend like her, especially in our darkest moments. We need someone who refuses to give us easy answers to make us feel better and who is fully present with us in our pain. This is my advice: Find a friend like Ruth, and just as important, be a friend like her.

We live in an instant society, but spiritual and emotional healing seldom comes in a flash. Be realistic about it, and commit yourself to the glory and the grind of healing the wounds in your life. Counselors tell us that we can expect a more or less predictable process of grieving our losses:

denial

recognition of our disappointments and wounds

anger at those who hurt us

bargaining to resolve the pain immediately

profound sadness when bargaining doesn't work

acceptance of the pain, process, and benefits of grief

Centuries ago, spiritual leaders listed despair as one of the chief sins of mankind. When we hear this, most of us react, "That's not fair. Individuals may not have sinned to cause their hurt at all!" But that's not the point. Disappointment and hurt aren't sin, but despair is the unwillingness to look to God, to gain his perspective on our problems, and to take courageous steps toward healing. Despair, then, is saying no to God, and for that reason, the ancients called it a sin.

I certainly don't want to be harsh or condemning, just objective. We can easily complain, blame others, and feel sorry for ourselves, and goodness knows, some of us have plenty to complain about! But

God wants us to look up, to see him in all of his wisdom, strength, and love, and to let him give us eyes of faith in the midst of our problems. Sometimes he rescues us out of them, but more often, he makes us shine like lights so others can see in the darkness.

How do we keep from despair? Look what happened when the Jewish leaders tried to persecute the disciples: "When they saw the courage of Peter and John and realized that they were unschooled, ordinary men, they were astonished and they took note that these men had been with Jesus."

As you read this book and move forward in your busy days ahead, spend time with Jesus. I know that sounds cliché, but it matters! Figure out what works for you. Is it reading a devotional? Spending quiet time in a chair at home talking with him or reading your Bible? Maybe it's a walk in the woods. Or a car ride with the worship music blaring. When you spend time with Jesus, the daily tasks will ease, and though you still need appreciation from others, you'll find that "life to the full" is found in time spent with him. Besides, you become like the people you spend time with.

Do you recognize yourself in this chapter? When you look in the mirror, do you see the sunken, hollow look of profound sadness? If this is what you see, ask God to help you see him more clearly.

Do you recognize a friend or family member in the description of sadness? Be a friend like Ruth. Offer your presence more than your advice, and be there as your friend musters the courage to take steps toward God's healing.

Healing the Damage

1. What are some differences between disappointment and despair?

2. What are the genuine threats in an abusive relationship? What keeps women hooked into these relationships? (What are their false beliefs about themselves, about God, about their abusers, and about their ability to make good choices?)

3. What are some negative stresses you've experienced in the past six months to a year? What are some positive changes that have produced stress? If you were an outside observer, how would you analyze your level of stress today?

4. Read Ruth 1. Describe the depth and intensity of Naomi's despair. Have you ever felt this hopeless, pushing people away when they tried to comfort and help you? How did it turn out?

5. Read Hebrews 4:14-16. When we are sad, why do we need to know that Jesus understands exactly how we feel?

6. Which of the steps at the end of the chapter do you (or a friend you want to help) need most at this point? What steps can you take to experience God's comfort?

7. In what ways is courage an essential part of the emotional and spiritual healing process?

8. Describe how a heart of faith helps women deal with disappointment.

"Beloved, never avenge yourselves, but leave it to the wrath of God, for it is written, 'Vengeance is mine, I will repay, says the Lord'" (Romans 12:19 ESV).

"But I say to you, Love your enemies and pray for those who persecute you" (Matthew 5:44 ESV).

"Come to me, all who labor and are heavy laden, and I will give you rest. Take my yoke upon you, and learn from me, for I am gentle and lowly in heart, and you will find rest for your souls. For my yoke is easy, and my burden is light" (Matthew 11:28-30 ESV).

"Then Peter came up and said to him, 'Lord, how often will my brother sin against me, and I forgive him? As many as seven times?' Jesus said to him, 'I do not say to you seven times, but seventy times seven.

"'Therefore the kingdom of heaven may be compared to a king who wished to settle accounts with his servants. When he began to settle, one was brought to him who owed him ten thousand talents. And since he could not pay, his master ordered him to be sold, with his wife and children and all that he had, and payment to be made'" (Matthew 18:21-25 ESV).

"The LORD appeared to him from far away. I have loved you with an everlasting love; therefore I have continued my faithfulness to you" (Jeremiah 31:3 ESV).

The *Flame* of *Anger*

Anger is an acid that can do more harm to the vessel in
which it is stored than to anything on which it is poured.

MARK TWAIN

Seven thirty-four Monday morning.

"Zach! We're gonna be late," I prodded. "Grab your cereal
bowl, and let's go!"

He scurried up the stairs, balancing a bowlful of cereal and
milk. With one hand, he let himself out of the house and into the
car, grabbed his seat belt, and buckled himself in. I threw the car
in drive, and off we went—me with a huge sigh and Zach with a
mouthful of cereal. I do *not* like being late!

As I drove out of our development, I mentally plotted a course
that would get us to Zach's school on time: *There's an opening on
Route 811. Maybe I could make my way over to I-460 instead of taking
I-501...*I decided to try the shortcut, exited onto Route 811, and sud-
denly saw—to my utter frustration—a sign that said, "Construction
Ahead. Lanes Merge." *Ugh!*

Zach's relaxed pace around the house earlier that morning and
now this road construction were more than my normally positive attitude could handle. Christian women don't get mad, right?
Guess again.

Thinking about anger brings back a lot of memories from my
first few years as a married woman. Tim and I were so young and

foolish that we became masters at hurting each other and making each other angry.

Some people get wild mad. Did you know that 7.3 percent of Americans (almost 16 million people) experience "intermittent explosive disorder" in their lifetimes?[1] This disorder is marked by episodes of unwarranted anger. I hope you are not married to someone with IED. Here are more interesting statistics on angry, rude, and hostile behavior:

1. One research poll shows that 78 percent of Americans think rude and selfish behavior is worse at airports and highways.[2]

2. We see incidents of road rage, air rage, cell-phone rage, checkout rage, bike rage, sports rage, parking rage, rail rage, bank rage, roller rage, boat rage, desk rage, car-alarm rage, and drivers who even honk at people on crutches. One expert has even identified "funeral rage" as people actually make obscene gestures and cut off funeral processions.[3]

3. Three out of four Americans say our manners are worse today than 20 or 30 years ago.[4]

4. Eighty-five percent of Americans believe the world would be a better place if we just said *please* and *thank you* more often.[5]

5. In a national survey of anger in the workplace, 42 percent of respondents said yelling and verbal abuse took place where they worked. Twenty-nine percent admitted that they themselves had yelled at coworkers. Thirty-four percent had suffered insomnia because of a stress-filled or anger-charged workplace. Eleven percent said they consumed excessive alcohol and 16 percent smoked too much for the same reasons.[6]

6. Nearly 25 percent of American workers suffer chronic anger on the job. Workplace anger is on the upswing because people feel betrayed by their employers.[7]

7. Twenty percent of American workers (139.4 million people) have suffered at the hands of bullies, and in 41 percent of the workplace incidents, the trauma was severe enough to warrant a clinical diagnosis of depression.[8]

8. Had it to here with rude drivers? One prominent study revealed that 90 percent of drivers experienced an aggressive driving incident.[9]

9. Drivers who tailgate, exceed speed limits, run red lights, and switch lanes with no warning contribute to the more than 6 million crashes each year in America.[10]

10. "Sideline rage" (parents behaving badly at youth sports events) is such an epidemic that 76 percent of respondents from 60 high school athletic associations said increased spectator interference is causing many officials to quit.[11]

11. In 2007, law enforcement agencies in the United States made an estimated 2.18 million arrests of persons under age 18.[12]

12. Violence affects the quality of life of young people who experience it, witness it, or feel threatened by it. Violence not only physically harms young victims but also adversely affects their mental health and development and increases the likelihood that they themselves will commit acts of serious violence. Youth ages 12 to 17 are twice as likely as adults to be victims of serious violent crimes including aggravated assault, rape, robbery (by force or threat of violence), and homicide.[13]

13. Are students morally adrift? Cheating in school continues to be rampant and it's getting worse. A substantial majority (64 percent) cheated on a test during the past year (38 percent did so two or more times), up from 60 percent and 35 percent, respectively, in 2006. In addition, more than eight in ten students (83 percent) from public schools and religious private schools confessed they lied to a parent about something significant.[14]

14. According to an online victimization study of 24 million kids between 10 and 17 who were online regularly in 1999, 6 million received sexually explicit material they didn't want, nearly 5 million were sexually solicited, and more than 1.4 million were harassed.[15]

15. Aggression is often learned at an early age. The aggressive schooltime behavior of an eight-year-old is an accurate indicator of how aggressive that child will be in adolescence and adulthood. That is why prevention programs that start early in childhood and continue through adolescence have the best chance for success.

The scary part about anger is that it always finds an expression. If it is not controlled, it can result in a cutting remark from a dear friend, an inappropriate gesture from a driver, or a no-show by a friend who is so mad at you that she doesn't even call or offer an explanation. Unexpressed anger can also be turned inward and cause other problems, like a critical spirit. You may have heard people say that anger turned inward is depression. How does this work?

One dictionary defines anger as "a strong feeling of displeasure and belligerence aroused by a wrong." Anger really is a God-given emotion in response to a real or perceived injustice or wrongdoing.

When we feel cheated or have been violated in some way, we often become angry. Regardless of what you may have been taught, feeling angry is not wrong. Rather, we are likely to cause even more problems if we don't allow ourselves to feel anger when it arises. The Bible doesn't tell us not to be angry. Rather, it says, "In your anger do not sin" (Ephesians 4:26). Anger isn't the problem. The way we manage our anger is the real issue.

Three of the ways we express our anger are unhealthy. When somebody hurts us, our immediate reaction may be to seek revenge. Some people are aggressive and yell and may even physically attack those who hurt them.

Other people express their anger passive-aggressively. Instead of directly confronting the people who wrong them, they decide that slashing their car tires would send a nice message. Gossiping, spreading rumors, and manipulating are also very common ways people strike back at those who have wronged them.

Dealing with our anger passively is also not good. Remember, anger always finds an expression, and if we turn anger inward, we take it out on ourselves, beating ourselves up for the anger we feel toward others. When we have been hurt, we want to make the wrong right again. But we can't control the situations or the other people, so we begin feeling guilty for not being able to fix it. This type of behavior usually leads to depression.

> Holding anger is a poison...It eats you from inside...We think that by hating someone we hurt them...But hatred is a curved blade...and the harm we do to others...we also do to ourselves.
> MITCH ALBOM

From time to time I meet women whose faces send mixed signals. They have beautiful smiles that communicate joy and thankfulness, but the look in their eyes tells a very different story. Instead of happiness, I see the hardened look of anger.

- Bethany is known for being quick-witted and cynical, and she constantly has a sarcastic smirk on her face. Under the smirk, though, lurks anger at those who hurt her.

- Nicole seemed to always be straining to keep a lid on her rage. She was like a volcano, smoldering under the surface and ready to blow any minute! Her anger, however, was coupled with fear of what might happen when the molten lava exploded on those around her.

- Carol's sour disposition left a permanent scowl on her face. The lines around her mouth were a sign that she lived each day gritting her teeth and daring anyone to cross her.

- Missy used her vicious glare to put everyone around her on guard—including me. I never knew how to act or what to say to her. She almost always overreacted to situations, so I assume a lot was going on under the surface.

- Many women I've met have smiling lips but angry eyes. They think they're hiding their true feelings of disappointment and outrage, but one look in their eyes reveals the truth.

Do you recognize anybody in those brief descriptions? When we read them, faces may flash in our minds, or we may feel as if we're looking in the mirror.

When Anger Helps and When It Hurts

Some Christians believe that anger is always wrong, but surely the issue is not that simple. Anger at injustice is good and right, and in fact, something is wrong with us if we don't feel angry when someone is abused or betrayed. Paul told his converts, "Your attitude should be the same as that of Christ Jesus" (Philippians

2:5). Jesus is our supreme example of humility and strength. He invites us to follow him, and we quickly realize that following him involves valuing the things he values, caring for the people he cares for, and working with him to advance the kingdom. When we read the Gospels, we see him healing the sick, raising the dead, calming storms, and feeding the hungry. But we also get glimpses of his frustration and anger—especially when he went to the temple and found people who were using it to oppress people and not to worship. John paints the picture for us:

> When it was almost time for the Jewish Passover, Jesus went up to Jerusalem. In the temple courts he found men selling cattle, sheep and doves, and others sitting at tables exchanging money. So he made a whip out of cords, and drove all from the temple area, both sheep and cattle; he scattered the coins of the moneychangers and overturned their tables. To those who sold doves he said, "Get these out of here! How dare you turn my Father's house into a market!" (John 2:13-16).

Can you imagine the scene? Jesus didn't just stamp his foot in disgust and walk out. He boldly spoke the truth and took action to change the situation. As we follow him, we will also have opportunities to act in righteous anger. When we see people suffer abuse, we won't just shake our heads in sad but impotent disapproval. We'll speak the truth to comfort the abused and confront the abuser, and we'll take appropriate action to protect the helpless and prevent further abuse.

Does this scenario seem far-fetched? You undoubtedly know friends and family members who suffer from emotional, physical, or sexual abuse. Even in Christian homes, the incidence of abuse is alarming. In fact, a study by Dr. Nancy Nason-Clark found that 28 percent of Christian marriages contain physical violence, and 50 to 56 percent contain abuse in some form.[16] Remember, that's just in Christian homes. Most of us feel safe and distant from worldwide problems like sex slave trafficking, but authorities estimate that there may be 27 million slaves today, more than at any other time in history. Women are sold by their families or are kidnapped into the sex slave trade. When we peel back the layer of ignorance and find out what these women endure, we should respond the same way Jesus did in the temple.[17]

And of course, many other causes call for our time and resources to help those in need. Bob Pierce, the founder of World Vision, clearly understood the right response to injustice. He wrote, "Let my heart be broken by the things that break the heart of God." Compassion is a powerful blend of outrage at injustice and loving action to help those who suffer—including ourselves when we are victims of abuse or abandonment.

> Anger is one letter short of danger.
> ANONYMOUS

Destructive Anger

When Paul wrote the believers in Ephesus, he instructed them, "In your anger do not sin" (Ephesians 4:26). We can infer by this passage that not all anger is sinful. As we've seen from Jesus' example, anger is sometimes a noble and measured response to injustice. However, most of us would probably admit that more often than not, we get angry not because of injustice, but because things and people get in the way of our own selfish motives.

Consider my own "road frustration" that I mentioned at the beginning of this chapter. How often do we get mad at other people on the road when the real problem is our own irresponsibility and tardiness? Think about how often we get angry with someone who obstructs our path, whether we are looking for the quickest check-out line at the grocery store or the quickest way to advance in our careers. Many of us also lash out in anger or simmer in discontent when we feel confused, threatened, or out of control.

The Scriptures and world history contain countless stories of anger and revenge.

- Cain murdered his brother, Abel, because Abel's sacrifice was better than his.

- Matthew Murray, a 24-year-old gunman, killed four people at a megachurch in Colorado because he was kicked out a few years earlier.

- Maria, a beautiful 28-year-old bride of three years, slept with her best friend's brother in an act of revenge against her husband after his remorseful admittance of prior infidelity.

- Laura started a rumor that Pam was a sleaze who slept with many men, because Pam started dating Laura's ex-boyfriend.

- A gang tortured and brutally beat Michael, an 18-year-old honor student, because he failed to acknowledge them as he walked past them on his way home from school.

In bedrooms and boardrooms and on the streets, demanding people hurt others and open the door for retaliation. Anger and revenge seem to be staples in our culture.

These types of anger show how far human nature has fallen, and they are terribly destructive, especially if we don't address them promptly. They never remain static; they grow foul and fester, egging us on toward revenge.

Of course, we Christian ladies never want to appear to be vicious, so we use gossip and other passive-aggressive weapons to punish others. Does that surprise you? It shouldn't. Gossip is simply a veiled attempt to take revenge—to hurt someone surreptitiously while we appear completely innocent. Think about it. Maybe you'll see it the same way and refuse to participate in it from now on.

In his New Testament letter, James didn't mince words about inordinate anger:

> My dear brothers, take note of this: Everyone should be quick to listen, slow to speak and slow to become angry, for man's anger does not bring about the righteous life that God desires. Therefore, get rid of all moral filth and the evil that is so prevalent and humbly accept the word planted in you, which can save you (James 1:19-21).

You might wonder, *When people make unrealistic demands, don't they act unjustly? Don't those situations call for righteous anger?* Well, yes, but if righteous anger isn't expressed appropriately and quickly, it morphs into bitterness and revenge. Whatever its source, anger is like a pot of hot liquid on the stoves of our lives. We need to handle it very carefully, but handle it we must.

Job's Beloved

Talk about getting a raw deal! Like a lightning bolt out of the blue, Job had no idea what hit him. For many years, he walked with God and enjoyed God's blessings, but suddenly everything fell apart, and he didn't have a clue what led to the change. Two bands of raiders stole part of his livestock and killed the servants who tended them. A messenger came to report that "fire from heaven" had killed the remaining sheep and the shepherds. Almost in the same breath, another rushed in to tell Job that a tornado had killed all of his children.

Stop for a minute. Allow that to sink in. You just lost all of your wealth—everything you have owned—as well as your only means for getting back on your feet. You are in utter shock, but the bad news not only keeps coming but also gets worse: All your beloved children have been killed!

In this moment of intense agony, Job didn't rage, curse people, or go after somebody. Rather, he reflected on God's goodness and sovereignty:

Naked I came from my mother's womb,
and naked I will depart.
The LORD gave and the LORD has taken away;
may the name of the LORD be praised (Job 1:21).

But the hits kept coming. As he grieved the loss of everything he owned and his dear children, Satan inflicted him with painful boils from his head to his feet. Even now, Job, devoid of the joys of his life and the safety and security of his God-given possessions, trusted God as he sat in ashes of sorrow and scraped his boils with a piece of pottery. At this poignant moment, Job needed warmth and understanding from someone who loved him, but Mrs. Job growled, "Are you still holding on to your integrity? Curse God and die!" (Job 2:9).

She could have said, "Honey, this is really confusing to me."

She could have told him, "My dear, no matter what happens, I'll always be with you."

Or she could have given him a huge hug and sat down beside him in the ashes without saying a word.

What would you have said or done?

Job's wife chose a different reaction, one I think every one of us as women need to honestly admit isn't too far from our own heart. She responded to her loss, to feeling utterly out of control, and to her husband's steadfast faith by attacking him and God. Can you picture the look in her eyes at that instant? In that crucial moment in their marriage and their individual lives, her heart screamed, *Give up!* She lashed out, blamed God, and left Job feeling completely abandoned.

We get yet another glimpse of Job's rock-solid faith in his measured response to his wife's attack. He told her, "You are talking like a foolish woman. Shall we accept good from God, and not trouble?" Now imagine how Job's wife feels. Her husband is not only insensitive to how this is affecting her, he is actually sticking up for God! Do you think she's honestly going to stop beating her husband up over this? Certainly not when she feels as if he is ignoring her own pain.

The contrast between Job's reaction and his wife's reaction is like night and day. But we have to admit, we often act more like Job's wife than like Job. Put yourself in her shoes. How would you feel if you lost *everything*—including your children—and your husband chose to talk only about God's sovereign right to dish out trouble.

This story reveals that we don't have to get angry when we face difficulties. We can cling to God and trust in his matchless wisdom even when we don't know what he's doing.

Fresh Insights

Some of us simply react to situations and people without thinking. We bounce from circumstance to circumstance and person to person, gravitating toward those who make us feel good and getting mad at those with whom we feel threatened. A moment of thought, though, can give us a fresh perspective about our reactions.

Some of us are a little too in touch with our emotions. All our feelings are on high alert all the time. We love intensely, but we also get angry with all our hearts. We have no problem being honest about our emotions. But many others feel quite threatened by anything but the most pleasant and benign feelings. Perhaps we were taught that anger is always sinful, so we've completely repressed it, or maybe we're afraid that if we open Pandora's box of rage in our hearts, the explosion would take months to clean up—if it could ever be cleaned up. It's crucial, though, for us to be aware of our emotions. We can enjoy the pleasant ones, and we can see the painful ones as flashing lights on the dashboard of our hearts.

Anger is a powerful emotion, so what I say now may seem odd to you: Most anger is a secondary, surface emotion. Unless it is righteous indignation toward injustice, it is most often fueled by underlying hurt and fear. If we don't uncover these sources, and if we simply try to keep a lid on our anger, the pressure will just keep rising until we explode.

Think about it. Women in loveless marriages express their anger, but below the surface they are tragically hurt and afraid of never being loved again. Many children and adolescents who lash out in anger are also hurt and afraid, but facing these emotions makes them feel even more vulnerable, so they express their anger instead.

Our anger is often tangled up with self-pity because we're sure we didn't get what we deserve. Nothing is wrong with feeling sorry for ourselves when we're disappointed, but left unchecked, our sadness can consume our thoughts, cloud our minds, and distort all our relationships, including our relationship with God.

We can't avoid feelings of anger, but we can choose how we express it—by pursuing resolution or by seeking revenge. Resolution is based on insight, so we desperately need God to open the eyes of our hearts so we can see circumstances and people the way God sees them. Insight helps us peel back the layers to uncover the hurt and fear that led to our anger.

Resolving our anger includes a healthy measure of forgiveness— not excusing the person who hurt us or minimizing the pain we feel, but choosing to avoid taking revenge by lashing out, punishing, withdrawing, or gossiping. Paul wrote in two of his letters that the benchmark for our forgiveness of those who hurt us is Christ's unmeasured forgiveness of us. The more we grasp his grace toward us and bask in his forgiveness for our sins, the more we'll be willing to forgive those who offend us. Paul wrote, "Get rid of all bitterness, rage and anger, brawling and slander, along with every form of malice. Be kind and compassionate to one another, forgiving each other, just as in Christ God forgave you" (Ephesians 4:31-32).

Some women's hearts are consumed with bitterness. Bitterness is always damaging and never helpful; it is anger that has festered and poisoned the soul. It is one of the greatest causes of emotional, spiritual, and relational pain in our lives. It ruins relationships, consumes our thoughts, saps our creativity, and causes psychosomatic illnesses.

Bitterness can always be traced to a beginning point. Some people's anger began after horrific abuse, and their anger was just and reasonable. But others simply didn't like someone getting in the way of their selfish goals, and their anger gradually turned sour. A person might ask, if bitterness is so destructive, why don't we recognize it and get rid of it immediately? The reason is that bitterness gives us three things we value:

an identity

energy

control through intimidation

Bitter people are convinced they have been wronged and therefore deserve special attention. Intense feelings of bitterness and the desire for revenge release endorphins in the brain and give us energy to make it through each day. And perhaps the most tangible "benefit" of bitterness is its power to intimidate those around us, making us feel powerful and enabling us to get our way. These reasons may seem attractive to some of us, but bitterness poisons every aspect of our lives. Author Lewis Smedes wrote extensively about the power of forgiveness. In an article for *Christianity Today*, he noted, "To forgive is to set a prisoner free and discover that the prisoner was you."[18]

> Speak when you are angry, and you'll make
> the best speech you'll ever regret.
> DR. LAURENCE PETER

Steps Forward

Have you ever been praying at home or sitting in church when suddenly, a troubling thought came into your mind about an unresolved disagreement between you and a friend? When this happens to me, I often want to simply shove the thought away so I can continue my nice conversation with the Lord. Yet inevitably, memories of harsh words and hurt feelings do not go away when I am communing with God, who is the light. He always seems to leave me to the troubling thoughts of the distressing situation.

At times, I have become frustrated and told God so. *Lord, please take these negative thoughts away. I really want to spend time with You right now.* But as I continue my walk with the Lord, I learn more about the importance of reconciliation prior to worship.

Jesus' Sermon on the Mount includes this radical statement:

> "Do not murder." I'm telling you that anyone who is so much as angry with a brother or sister is guilty of murder. Carelessly call a brother "idiot!" and you just might find yourself hauled into court. Thoughtlessly yell "stupid!" at a sister and you are on the brink of hellfire. The simple moral fact is that words kill.
>
> This is how I want you to conduct yourself in these matters. If you enter your place of worship and, about to make an offering, you suddenly remember a grudge a friend has against you, abandon your offering, leave immediately, go to this friend and make things right. Then and only then, come back and work things out with God (Matthew 5:21-24 MSG).

Does anyone come to mind whom you have wronged or who has wronged you? Someone you're angry at? If so, now may be the time to follow Jesus' mandate in Matthew 5. Go to that brother or sister, do all you can to be reconciled, and return to worshipping the Lord. Only then will you truly experience the full experience of communion with God.

God made us relational creatures. Surely our relationship with him is connected to our relationship with those around us. However, reconciliation does not always come easily and cannot be done alone. In order to walk uprightly in the Lord, we need at least one other mature, caring believer to help us work through our anger. This friend, counselor, or group invites us to be honest about the anger we feel (or have been reluctant to feel) so we can dig beneath the surface to find the source. The process of discovery may take only an instant, or it may require serious excavation. Sometimes I encourage ladies to spend time alone with a pen and paper and ask God's Spirit to reveal painful and fearful moments in their past.

To do this, give yourself plenty of time. The process is too important and too powerful to be rushed. Quite often, a first wave of memories comes in a flash. You may not remember anything more for a while, but after a while, thoughts you haven't had in a long time begin to surface. Sometimes these don't even make sense, but write them down anyway. The pieces might come together later. And usually, after even more time, a few long-buried memories bubble up.

After women have done this exercise, many have told me, "I hadn't thought of that event in years, but now I realize how it has shaped my life since the day it happened." The memories may be traumatic, or they may show the emptiness of abandonment. Regardless of what God's Spirit brings to your mind, each moment from the past is a piece of your life puzzle. As you talk about these with a trusted friend, work hard to identify these deep, hidden sources of hurt and moments of fear. They are the wellsprings of today's anger.

One of the most important lessons of life is that we can choose the direction of our lives by attending to our thoughts and actions. In the past, we may have simply reacted without thinking, but no longer. Of course, we can't keep all negative thoughts out of our minds, but we can recognize them and replace them with positive ones.

> Finally, brothers, whatever is true, whatever is noble, whatever is right, whatever is pure, whatever is lovely, whatever is admirable—if anything is excellent or praiseworthy—think about such things. Whatever you have learned or

received or heard from me, or seen in me—put it into practice. And the God of peace will be with you (Philippians 4:8-9).

When you see or hear of injustice, let your righteous anger motivate you to take constructive action to right the wrongs. And when you feel threatened, when you feel out of control, or when someone blocks your selfish goals, recognize your feelings and choose to think rightly. Reflect on the passages in this chapter. Memorize them and use them to guide your thinking.

And choose to forgive. Author Philip Yancey calls forgiveness "the unnatural act" because everything in us cries out for revenge. Don't give in to those negative impulses. As Paul instructed the Ephesians, think long and hard about the price Christ paid to forgive you, and let that insight sink deep into your heart to produce gratitude and the willingness to forgive those who hurt you.

> Forgiveness is the oil of relationships.
> JOSH MCDOWELL

Forgiving others, however, doesn't imply that you should trust those who have hurt you. We forgive because God has commanded us to forgive and because forgiveness frees us from the bondage of bitterness, but we are foolish to trust untrustworthy people. We offer forgiveness unilaterally and freely, but trust must be earned.

When we deal with our anger, we uncover hidden and sometimes excruciating wounds and terrors. We face those events and grieve our losses and pain, and God walks with us through the valley of the shadow of death. As we take those courageous steps, the look in our eyes may shift from an angry glare to tears of sadness, but this detour is only temporary. Genuine grief frees us from the hurts of the past just as forgiving sets us free from bitterness.

We don't face the demons in our past alone. We have friends who will walk with us, and Jesus has promised that he'll never leave us or forsake us. Regardless of how confused we feel, he's right beside us every step of the way. Ask him to fill you with courage to face the truth about what caused you so much pain, and trust him to give you more wisdom, joy, peace, and love than you've ever felt before.

Our faces need not be stuck in scowls, smirks, or glares. When we forgive one another from our hearts, the lines around our eyes soften, and we sense God's presence, peace, and purpose.

Healing the Damage

1. How would you describe the various looks of anger in women's eyes? Do you see any of these when you look in the mirror? Explain your answer.

2. Read John 2:13-17. Describe some differences between righteous anger and selfish anger.

3. Why is it significant that Ephesians 4:26 assumes we will be angry?

4. Think of someone who was stuck in bitterness. In what way did his or her bitterness provide identity, energy, and control?

5. Is anger a surface emotion that covers hurt and fear? Explain your answer.

6. As you look at the Steps Forward at the end of the chapter, do you need to take any of these steps? If so, write a plan of how you will take them. Who is the trusted friend you'll talk with about what you discover?

========= Bible Passages on Anger =========

"May the words of my mouth and the meditation of my
    heart be pleasing in your sight,
    O LORD, my Rock and my Redeemer" (Psalm 19:14).

"'In your anger do not sin': Do not let the sun go down
while you are still angry, and do not give the devil a
foothold" (Ephesians 4:26-27).

"When Moses approached the camp and saw the calf
and the dancing, his anger burned and he threw the
tablets out of his hands, breaking them to pieces at the
foot of the mountain" (Exodus 32:19).

"When I heard their outcry and these charges, I was very
angry" (Nehemiah 5:6).

"Do not make friends with a hot-tempered man,
    do not associate with one easily angered,
or you may learn his ways
    and get yourself ensnared" (Proverbs 22:24-25).

"How the Lord has covered the Daughter of Zion
    with the cloud of his anger!
He has hurled down the splendor of Israel
    from heaven to earth;
he has not remembered his footstool
    in the day of his anger" (Lamentations 2:1).

"But God said to Jonah, 'Do you have a right to be angry
    about the vine?'
"'I do,' he said. 'I am angry enough to die'" (Jonah 4:9).

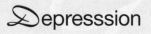epresssion

That's the thing about depression: A human being
can survive almost anything, as long as she sees
the end in sight. But depression is so insidious, and
it compounds daily, that it's impossible to ever see
the end. The fog is like a cage without a key.

ELIZABETH WURTZEL

*K*ara seemed to have it all. Smart and attractive, she worked her way up the corporate ladder, attaining respect and a prominent position. Her husband had also achieved success in his career. Together they shared a comfortable lifestyle and a seemingly happy marriage. Several years ago, Kara gave birth to her first child—a little girl—and all seemed to be perfect for them.

Kara's friends admired her for various reasons. She could seemingly do it all, balancing a demanding career with family time, volunteer work, community projects, exercise, and church involvement. Her home was decorated and landscaped beautifully and maintained immaculately. Kara was always impeccably dressed and took pride in her personal appearance.

But the first time I met Kara, something was clearly terribly wrong. She looked completely exhausted and made no attempt to brighten her appearance in any way. As soon as we began talking, she burst into tears.

Between bouts of crying, she was able to explain the devastating symptoms that finally compelled her to seek help. In the few weeks prior, she had lost a significant amount of weight, had trouble falling asleep, felt totally exhausted, and was easily agitated and highly irritable.

> One of the most tragic things I know about human nature
> is that all of us tend to put off living. We are all dreaming
> of some magical rose garden over the horizon instead of
> enjoying the roses blooming outside our windows today.
>
> DALE CARNEGIE

What Is Depression?

The emptiness, despair, and sadness that Kara described are symptoms of depression, which now affects 10 to 25 percent of women and 5 to 12 percent of men annually. And the American Psychological Association has discovered that major depressive disorder is twice as common in adolescent and adult females as in adolescent and adult males.[1]

Kara's problem was not difficult to understand given the symptoms. She was suffering from postpartum depression, a disorder affecting 10 to 15 percent of women within their first year following childbirth.[2]

If you have ever attended an Extraordinary Women conference, you have heard Chonda Pierce tell her testimony of being hospitalized because of her depression. As a result she helped found Branches Recovery Center, a respite to aid those suffering from depression and other recovery issues.

Some of history's most well-respected leaders struggled with depression, including Winston Churchill, Martin Luther, and Abraham Lincoln.

Jonah was overcome with sadness when his prophecy of Nineveh's destruction did not come to pass. Depressed and weary, Elijah asked God to take his life. Jeremiah and Job both wished they had never been born. More recent church leaders have also struggled with depression, including John Bunyan and Charles Spurgeon.

Pressures from the past and present can weigh us down. So can physical issues, such as hormonal changes, menstruation, pregnancy, and childbirth. These can leave us feeling shortchanged and longing for more energy, stamina, and hope so we can enjoy life. But in the meantime, we may remained paralyzed and left feeling as though life is not the way it's supposed to be.

Signs of depression include sadness, hopelessness, pessimism, difficulty in making decisions, general fatigue, a loss of energy, and a lack of interest in work, sex, religion, hobbies, or other activities. No wonder just getting out of bed in the morning is such a daunting task! Those suffering from depression may also experience low self-esteem and feelings of guilt, shame, and worthlessness. A loss of spontaneity, insomnia, excessive crying, irritability, and loss of appetite are also common symptoms. Of the nine criteria mentioned above used to clinically diagnose depression, only four are needed.

Depressions are best viewed from a holistic perspective because they affect the way we think, feel, behave, and relate. We feel upset not only emotionally but also physically. These episodes are not simply the temporary blues or the passing sad moods that everyone experiences after a loss. Depression can interfere with people's ability to function at work, and in more severe forms, it can hinder people from getting out of bed or eating. More than 90 percent of people who die by suicide have depressive symptoms.[8]

CATEGORIES OF DEPRESSION
Major Depressive Episode—Five or more symptoms in the same two-week period. One of the symptoms must be either 1. depressed mood most of the day or nearly every day, or 2. markedly diminished interest or pleasure in activities most of the day or nearly every day.
Manic Episode—A distinct period of abnormally and persistently elevated, expansive, or irritable mood, lasting at least one week with three other symptoms coexisting (such as inflated self-esteem, decreased need for sleep, excessive talkativeness, flight of ideas or racing thoughts, distractibility, increase in goal-directed activity, and excessive involvement in activities with dangerous consequences).

This chart of the various types of clinical depression is from the *Diagnostic and Statistical Manual of Mental Disorders*.[4] Tim has explained to me how the different types of depression manifest themselves. As I just mentioned, depression is not the typical mood fluctuations or the feelings of sadness and disappointment we all feel from time to time—feelings that last only minutes to a few days. Clinical depression is more serious because it is not a now-and-again occurrence. It is more like a constant state for weeks or months or even years at a time.

As the text in the box mentions, one or more major depressive episodes must have occurred in order to diagnose major depression. You can distinguish major depression from a normal depressed mood by determining whether the mood has lasted two weeks or more, with a loss of interest in once enjoyable activities. In addition, four of the following must also be present:

> weight loss (not due to dieting), weight gain, or change in appetite
>
> insomnia or excessive sleep
>
> diminished movements or agitation

loss of energy or fatigue

feelings of worthlessness or inappropriate or excessive guilt

indecisiveness or an inability to concentrate

recurrent thoughts of death or suicide

Many women experience the more mild form of depression called dysthymic disorder. In these cases, the symptoms are not as serious as in major depression, but a depressed mood does exist most of the time for two years or more.

> My depression is the most faithful mistress I have known. No wonder, then, that I return the love.
> SØREN KIERKEGAARD

Reasons and Causes

Depression can be caused by several factors. Experts generally group these factors into six different categories:

biological and genetic influences (heredity)

physiological issues (such as poor diet, insomnia, tumors, and glandular disorders)

interpersonal factors (including strained relationships, divorce, or loss of a loved one)

spiritual causes (sin and suffering)

personality types (temperament, anger turned inward, loneliness, and so on)

environmental causes (such as an economic recession)

Have you seen a commercial advertising Pristiq, a depression medication? It opens with a woman turning the key in the back of a windup figurine. The windup doll is a woman with her head down who can barely move without the turn of the key. A woman's voice says, "Depression can make you feel like you have to wind yourself up to make it through the day..." The commercial goes on to explain the effects of depression and its causes: low levels of norepinephrine or serotonin, two chemicals needed for proper brain functioning. Commercials like this reveal biological and genetic influences that sometimes cause depression. Environmental issues and life stress could also make those who have lower levels of these chemicals more susceptible to depression.

Physiological issues that can lead to depression include a lack of sleep, improper diet, a lack of regular exercise, working too much, and exhaustion, especially for those who have taken good care of their bodies in the past. Physical disease and illness such as chronic pain, an underactive thyroid, a tumor, or a traumatic injury can alter people's lifestyles and precipitate feelings of depression. Two of the most common physiological causes include postpartum depression (which is a mixture of biological and physiological issues) and seasonal affective disorder. Postpartum depression creates a difficult struggle and affects about 10 percent of women within their first year after giving birth.[5] Seasonal affective disorder doesn't usually last as long and is limited to regions that experience winter months of clouds, cold weather, and dreariness.

Interpersonal factors can also cause depression. When a marriage is not working, it turns into a stressor that often causes depression in one or both spouses. A stressful marriage is the leading cause for depression among women.[6] Consistent conflict and criticism seem to contribute to relapses back into depression. Divorce, loss of a loved one (particularly a spouse), and dysfunctional families all increase the likelihood of depression.

Have you ever heard a pastor or church leader claim that depression is caused by a lack of faith or inconsistent Bible reading or prayer? Maybe someone told you this. If so, you probably felt even more depressed because you also felt guilty for not living up to God's alleged expectations for you.

Job's friends did this. When Job lost everything he held dear—his seven children, his wealth, and his health—his friends eventually accused him of not living up to the potential that God had for him. In effect, they told him that God would not allow such tragedy to happen to those who walk uprightly and without sin. Yet twice the Bible states that Job did not sin (Job 1:22; 2:10).

Depression can also have spiritual causes. Sin and its consequences can certainly lead to depressed feelings. But it's also important to understand that other factors besides a lack of faith or failure to read the Bible often play a role. Will a lack of faith or laziness in the spiritual disciplines make depression worsen? Usually. But they are almost never the lone cause.

That is not to say that personal sin does not cause depression. Think about the things mentioned in Galatians 5:19-21 and Colossians 3:5-10 that Paul tells us to rid ourselves of: bitterness, hatred, a guilty conscience, lack of repentance of sinful behaviors and attitudes, sexual immorality, idolatry, envy, drunkenness, jealousy, dissension, discord, impurity, malice, filthy language, greed, turning your back on God, not reading the Bible, fear of the future, lack of confidence that God will provide for you, and unbelief. Living constantly and consistently in any of these attitudes and behaviors will significantly increase the risk of depression because in the end, every one of them leaves you feeling emptier and more worthless than before. Nothing but God's grace and forgiveness will end the bondage and satisfy the deepest longings of your heart.

When trials and tribulations come, your confidence that God will fulfill the desires of your heart can help ward off depression. God used tragedy in Job's life to prune and purify his heart. Job approached his suffering with faith and trust that God would help him through the difficult time. Without such faith, he could have easily succumbed to depression. God often uses such trials to mold and shape us into his image (John 15:2; 1 Peter 1:6-7), but without this knowledge, we are susceptible.

Personality issues can also lead to depression. Difficult life experiences—like the loss of a parent through death or divorce—can make people susceptible to depression. Individuals who have suffered such trauma are much more prone to feel guilty even when they have done nothing wrong. They live with a sense that they are not worthy of love, so they avoid relational issues to keep from offending people and being abandoned.

Feelings of loneliness, especially among the elderly, can also cause depression. Early in the Bible, God said that it was not good for us to be alone (Genesis 2:18). Other precipitating factors of depression include rejection, insult, failure, success (especially if it becomes too stressful to handle), a lack of positive, fun-filled events and laughter, and the mind-set that you can't change a situation.

Depression is usually the result of several factors. Rarely is a single cause at the root of this complex and damaging emotion.

> It is better to light one small candle
> than to curse the darkness.
> ELEANOR ROOSEVELT

Women and Depression

Most people believe that women are at a much higher risk of depression than men. Several unique factors contribute to this risk. For example, women are more likely to live in poverty and suffer physical or sexual abuse. In addition, hormonal changes and transitions make women more susceptible to suffer from depression. These transitions include menarche, pregnancy, contraceptive usage, menstrual cycle, miscarriage, hysterectomy, oophorectomy, perimenopause, menopause, and hormone replacement therapy.

Biological factors are a major cause of depression in women:

Premenstrual syndrome (PMS). If a woman has severe premenstrual mood swings, depression, irritability, or anxiety (with or without physical symptoms), she is diagnosed as having premenstrual dysphoric disorder (PMDD). This severe type of PMS affects up to 8 percent of women.[7] Most women are able to face and effectively cope with these mood changes each month. However, some women are so affected by the hormonal changes that they feel ashamed, helpless, or out of control. When the mood shifts become serious enough to interfere with relationships and daily functioning, they can contribute to or cause depression.

Childbirth (postpartum depression). Mild postpartum depression includes crying spells, restlessness, and feelings of unreality and confusion. The overwhelming changes that come with motherhood are partially to blame, but hormonal shifts that occur seven to ten days following birth have been shown to contribute to this form of depression in women as well.

Menopause and the empty nest. As a woman ages, physical and emotional changes in her life can trigger episodes of intense sadness or serious depression. The psychological and physical changes of menopause clearly contribute to negative thoughts and struggles about self and life. The emotional effects and sudden lifestyle changes that occur when children leave the home can also be upsetting and cause turmoil in a woman's life.

A Depressed Prophet

Depression has a very subtle way of draining our energy and forcing us to question whether we can trust God to be there in our day-to-day lives. Even Elijah, one of Israel's greatest prophets who courageously confronted King Ahab and the false prophets of Baal (1 Kings 18:17-40), fell into a deep depression when Queen Jezebel threatened to kill him.

In fact, Elijah didn't even want to live anymore—hurting so badly he crawled up under a tree and asked God to let him die. The Bible records Elijah's symptoms of depression: He lost his appetite and his ability to think effectively, and he isolated himself from everyone around him. I am still amazed that a prophet like Elijah could have asked God to take his life. Even the great men and women of God we learned about in Sunday school as children struggled in their day-to-day lives.

Elijah was a brave man. But imagine if somebody was trying to track you down and threatened to kill you? I know I'd be scared! Elijah was—he responded in fear.

In fact, fear is prevalent in many kinds of depression—so much that anxiety coexists with depression in many cases. Proverbs 12:25 (NKJV) reveals, "Anxiety in the heart of man causes depression, but a good word makes it glad."

How would you expect God to respond to Elijah's depression? When you're depressed, how do you picture God? Judgmental? Angry? Upset? Wishing you would just get up and do something?

God was just the opposite with Elijah. He responded mercifully. He didn't criticize, reprimand, or condemn Elijah for feeling depressed. God did exactly what we need to do with others who are depressed (and with ourselves). He first took care of him physically by giving him food and rest. "Suddenly an angel touched him, and said to him, 'Arise and eat.' Then he looked, and there by his head was a cake baked on coals, and a jar of water. So he ate and drank, and lay down again" (1 Kings 19:5-6 NKJV). After a second serving of food and drink from an angel, Elijah "went in the strength of that food" (verse 8). Next, God encouraged Elijah to go, providing him with very specific instructions for what to do next. We should follow the same example in helping ourselves and others overcome depressed feelings.

God also focused on Elijah's bad thinking. Having isolated himself from the rest of the world, Elijah came to believe that he was the only faithful person left in Israel—but he wasn't. "Yet I have reserved seven thousand in Israel, all whose knees have not bowed to Baal, and every mouth that has not kissed him" (verse 18). So God sent Elijah to do what we all need to do when we're depressed, anxious, or otherwise self-absorbed—serve others. God sent Elijah to train Elisha, and this happened to be the remedy for Elijah's focus on himself and his depression.

Elijah walked through the valley of the shadow of death with God. He learned that God would never forsake him. Even when we are in the depths of depression, God shows us his loving concern and provides a way out.

<hr>

Steps Forward

Build awareness. Get the facts. Awareness is the first step in overcoming depression.

Deal with physical issues. If you suspect that a physical problem is causing you to struggle with depression, seek professional help immediately. One estimate suggests that 40 percent of depression may come as a result of physical illness. A complete physical examination and medical workup is in order. In addition, talk with your doctor about an exercise program. Research consistently shows that moderate exercise reduces the grip of depression.

Deal with negative thinking. Depressed people want to feel better, but their feelings are hard to change. The key is to change the negative thinking patterns often characteristic of depression. Philippians 4:8 gives us guidelines for editing our thought patterns.

Seek support. Depressed persons usually withdraw from friends, family, and church in order to get control of their lives or rest. This withdrawal may be logical, but it often isolates people from support and positive interactions. Maintaining a balance between rest, God time, interaction with others, and outside activities is important.

Psalm 46 was a powerful encouragement to Martin Luther in his depression. I encourage you to read it. Even in our distress, we can find God. In addition, a good support group can be of help.

Get outside help. Sometimes depressive disorders make people less willing or able to get help. Effective counseling treatments and medications are available, and they can improve your quality of life and prevent future relapses. Of those who seek help for severe depression, 80 percent are able to return to daily activities, usually within a matter of weeks. If you need help, don't be afraid to seek out a pastor, physician, or counselor.

Remember, your pain right now may seem stronger than any

hope for the future, but the burdens you are carrying need not be your burdens forever. Hope will return as you start to reach out for it—not by denying the present situation, but by knowing that even in the pain of today, there is hope for a better tomorrow.

Healing the Damage

1. As you read about depression and its effects, did any of the information seem to describe your life, either now or in the past?

2. When do you feel the most depressed? On the weekends? When your husband is away from home? During the holidays? In the morning?

3. Keep a journal of the times you feel the most depressed and see if any patterns emerge. This may give you clues about the circumstances that are most likely to trigger these feelings.

4. What symptoms of depression do you struggle with the most?

5. How have you attempted to overcome depressive feelings? What has worked for you, and what hasn't?

6. What else can you do to overcome depression?

Bible Passages on Depression

"Out of the depths I cry to you, O LORD;
  O Lord, hear my voice.
Let your ears be attentive
    to my cry for mercy.
If you, O LORD, kept a record of sins,
    O Lord, who could stand?

But with you there is forgiveness;
    therefore you are feared.
I wait for the LORD, my soul waits,
    and in his word I put my hope.
My soul waits for the Lord
    more than watchmen wait for the morning,
    more than watchmen wait for the morning.
O Israel, put your hope in the LORD,
    for with the LORD is unfailing love
    and with him is full redemption.
He himself will redeem Israel
    from all their sins" (Psalm 130).

"Why are you downcast, O my soul?
    Why so disturbed within me?
Put your hope in God,
    for I will yet praise him,
    my Savior and my God.
My soul is downcast within me;
    therefore I will remember you
from the land of the Jordan,
    the heights of Hermon—from Mount Mizar.
Deep calls to deep
    in the roar of your waterfalls;
all your waves and breakers
    have swept over me.
By day the LORD directs his love,
    at night his song is with me—
    a prayer to the God of my life.
I say to God my Rock,
    'Why have you forgotten me?
Why must I go about mourning,
    oppressed by the enemy?'
My bones suffer mortal agony
    as my foes taunt me,
saying to me all day long,

'Where is your God?'
Why are you downcast, O my soul?
    Why so disturbed within me?
Put your hope in God,
    for I will yet praise him,
        my Savior and my God" (Psalm 42:5-11).

"[He has sent me to] provide for those who grieve
        in Zion—
to bestow on them a crown of beauty
    instead of ashes,
the oil of gladness
    instead of mourning,
and a garment of praise
    instead of a spirit of despair.
They will be called oaks of righteousness,
    a planting of the LORD
    for the display of his splendor" (Isaiah 61:3).

"Though you have made me see troubles, many and bitter,
    you will restore my life again;
from the depths of the earth
    you will again bring me up" (Psalm 71:20).

"Great is your love toward me;
    you have delivered me from the depths of the grave"
    (Psalm 86:13).

"Is it nothing to you, all you who pass by?
    Look around and see.
Is any suffering like my suffering
    that was inflicted on me,
that the LORD brought on me
    in the day of his fierce anger?" (Lamentations 1:12).

"Neither height nor depth, nor anything else in all creation, will be able to separate us from the love of God that is in Christ Jesus our Lord" (Romans 8:39).

"Brothers, we do not want you to be ignorant about those who fall asleep, or to grieve like the rest of men, who have no hope" (1 Thessalonians 4:13).

Lust: Never Enough Love

Carnal lust rules where there is no love of God.
SAINT AUGUSTINE

How long has it been since you read the story of Cinderella or Snow White? Do you remember your childhood dreams of being a princess in a fairy tale? Perhaps you still hold to that dream (and a part of me hopes you do!). I remember sharing those feelings, imagining that I would be discovered and romanced because I was either long-lost royalty or the answer to a prince's longing for love and adventure. My heart swelled with delight as I imagined the prince taking my hand and my heart.

Imagine this scene with me. A beautiful heroine walks into a room, and all eyes rest on her. She is a little confused and embarrassed by the effect she has on the people around her. Her humble confidence radiates from her because she is simply being herself, authentically real and beautiful, with no agenda or desire to manipulate or entice others.

Who would not want to be a fairy-tale princess? Beautiful, alluring, loved, and saved by a dashing prince who lives to sweep her off her feet and offer her his kingdom.

Why do we have these dreams? Could it be because they hint at something true, something about the way God made us? Amid the deadlines, screaming babies, unpaid bills, and piles of laundry, something inside of you longs not only for rest but also for romance. Do you remember the last time you were surprised with a bouquet of flowers by that special man in your life? Even a clumsy attempt to woo you probably brought a smile to your face or maybe even a tear to your eye.

But if we go a long time without feeling pursued, we may try to fulfill our longings in any way we can—even by being a little "playful."

As I was working on this chapter, I struggled to think of good personal anecdotes about lust. I could tell you about my infatuation with Donny Osmond when he was in his prime. (In case you aren't yet 30, Donny Osmond was the Zac Efron of my teenage years.) I joined the Donny Osmond fan club and even wore the big pink socks. And yes, I followed him recently on *Dancing with the Stars*. Tim laughed.

But the more I thought about this chapter and the idea of lust, the more I thought about an interesting twist on the word itself. I understand the negative connotation of the word—sexual desire outside the boundaries of marriage. Jesus said that if we lust after another, we have already committed adultery in our hearts. That is a radical teaching in a culture like ours, where sex sells. Everywhere you look—television and movies, books and magazines, music and advertising—sexual images and messages scream at women to release the "wild child" within and use their sexual power to enhance their lives.

But what if I lust after God's Word? What if I lust after God's presence? What if I lust after my husband, Tim?

As I researched this idea a little more I found that the Hebrew word for *lust* means "to desire eagerly, to long for, to wish, to crave, to covet, to yearn, to be eager to, to have an appetite for." Even the Hebrew word for *covet* is defined as "to desire, lustful, be carnally excited in a pure way." But it also means "to have greed or avarice, to be grasping or envious." Consider the way Scripture uses these concepts in a positive sense (look up the verses in the NKJV):

In Isaiah 26:8, the desire of God's people is for God's name.

In Proverbs 13:12, fulfilled desire is called a tree of life.

In Psalm 19:7-10, David says the law of the Lord is more desirable than gold.

In Psalm 21:2, David praises God for giving him the desire of his heart.

In 1 Peter 1:12, angels desire to look into the gospel.

In Luke 17:22, Jesus said his disciples would long to see the Son of Man.

Pastor John Piper explains, "Sexual desire in itself is good. God made it in the beginning. It has its proper place. But it was made to be governed or regulated or guided by two concerns: honor toward the other person and holiness toward God."[1]

So is lust good or bad? It depends on your mind-set and heart.

Our culture has twisted our understanding of love and sex and spoiled our once-pure desire to be loved, held, and cherished. We sometimes cooperate in this process by letting our desires run wild and even inappropriately trying to fulfill them.

For some, this path leads to pornography. It's a huge issue for men, and women are not immune. Statistics now show that 70 percent of women are keeping their cyber activities secret, and 17 percent of women are struggling with pornography addiction. In addition, one in three visitors to adult websites is a woman, and 13 percent admit to accessing pornography at work.[2] And that includes only those who admitted it. Maybe you're wondering how anybody could get caught up in merely looking at an image in a magazine or on a computer. But consider this: How many of us are caught up in making sure we TiVo our daytime soap opera every day? Or addicted to daydreams about other men or other life situations?

Interestingly, romance novel sales are surging faster than sales of any other genre of book right now. A *Los Angeles Times* article, "The recession heats up romance novels," reported that even though sales in the general book market took a slight decrease in the fourth quarter of 2008, romance novels saw a $3 million gain from the previous year.[3] The irony (or the sad part, depending on how you look at it) is that readers of romance novels are more likely to be in a relationship than single, either married or cohabiting.

The Internet Filter Review reveals that...

- $3,075.64 is spent on pornography every second.
- 28,258 people view Internet pornography every second.
- 372 people type adult search terms into search engines every second.
- A new pornographic video is created in the United States every 39 minutes.[4]

And the Romance Writers of America report that...

- 74.8 million Americans read a romance novel in 2008. That's 24.6 percent of Americans, up from 21.8 percent in 2005.
- The romance fiction market has 29 million regular readers.
- 90.5 percent of the romance readers are women. Most of these are age 31 to 49 and are currently in a romantic relationship.[5]

You may think seductive women exist only in strip clubs or as the mistresses of wealthy and powerful men, but they're far more common than that. You see them in the mall, in the grocery store, and in restaurants. They even go to church and Extraordinary Women conferences. In fact, by the time you're finished reading this chapter you may realize you know more about the subject than you wanted to admit.

These women have "Bette Davis eyes"—a mixed look of seduction and confusion. Their eyes are windows into their hearts and reveal their consuming desire to heal the emptiness inside. Some people have described this as a God-shaped vacuum. And though it may be shaped for God, too many women are filling it with fantasies, idealistic dreams, or the right man rather than God. These women have learned the power of sex and sensuality to control and manipulate the men around them and numb their ache inside.

Make no mistake. Some Christians feel guilty about sexual desires and behaviors, but sex is God's good gift to be enjoyed to the fullest, and God isn't embarrassed about it at all. In fact, he created it. Song of Songs, a seldom-read portion of the Bible, probably because it is so descriptive and erotic, celebrates creativity and delight in a couple's sexual experience. In one passage, the lover describes his wife's beautiful body, her grace, and his delight in her:

> Your lips are like a scarlet ribbon;
>   your mouth is lovely.
> Your temples behind your veil
>   are like the halves of a pomegranate.
> Your neck is like the tower of David,
>   built with elegance;
> on it hang a thousand shields,
>   all of them shields of warriors.
> Your two breasts are like two fawns,
>   like twin fawns of a gazelle
>   that browse among the lilies.
> Until the day breaks
>   and the shadows flee,
> I will go to the mountain of myrrh
>   and to the hill of incense.
> All beautiful you are, my darling;
>   there is no flaw in you (Song of Songs 4:3-7).

The wife delights in her husband's advances as he explores every part of her body. Together, they enjoy creativity and sensuality in all their fullness as he "browses among the lilies." She compares him to an athletic young stag in making love:

My lover is mine and I am his;
    he browses among the lilies.
Until the day breaks
    and the shadows flee,
turn, my lover,
    and be like a gazelle
or like a young stag
    on the rugged hills (Song of Songs 2:16-17).

When dealing with misplaced sexual urges, the goal is not to repress them, but to see sexuality the way God intended it. Sex was his idea, and he is more than willing to guide us so we can enjoy that part of our lives. It is so powerful, though, that we need to handle it with extreme care.

Sexual Redemption

We may think that sexual sin and out-of-control lust are among the worst of all sins, but God seems to take pleasure in redeeming people who are considered outcasts by the rest of society. The Bible is full of stories of men and women with less than exemplary sex lives whom God forgave and restored in wonderful ways.

Rahab was a hooker in Jericho who protected the spies from Israel. Had she discovered that the true God was the God of Israel and not the idols her people worshipped? What was the measure of God's redemption in her life? She and her family were spared from destruction when the Israelite soldiers overran the city, but more significantly, we find Rahab in Matthew's record of Jesus' genealogy. She was the sexual sinner who experienced God's grace and became a link in the chain that led to the Savior.

Bathsheba is an interesting woman to consider in light of sexual sin. She was strikingly beautiful, but she was evidently less than discreet by bathing on the roof of her house in plain view of King David. He lusted for her, called her to the palace, and slept with her. I don't know if she protested, but I can imagine that she was intimidated by David's position and reputation. Later, the prophet Nathan confronted David about his sin of adultery and murder to cover up the sin. David repented, and he experienced God's cleansing. God's Messiah came from the lineage of David and Bathsheba. David was a powerful king who experienced not only the consequences of his lust but also God's healing and faithfulness to fulfill his purpose.

Jesus seemed to take special delight in reaching out to women in trouble. When he was reclining at a table in the home of a religious leader, a woman who had led a sinful life came to him and wet his feet with her tears, dried them with her hair, and poured perfume on them. The leader was terribly offended by the disreputable woman's presence in his home, but Jesus saw beyond her past behavior and into her heart. He forgave her and made her a new woman.

Jesus also offered forgiveness to the woman at the well and the woman caught in adultery. The first had had five sexual partners and was an outcast from her village. The second may have had countless partners, but this time, she was caught in the act. (Not a great way to start the day!) Jesus didn't distance himself from these needy ladies and condemn them. Others had already done that with no positive effect, but not Jesus. He stepped into their world, loved them, forgave them, and gave them the power to change the course of their lives.

The church may not talk much about sex, but it certainly isn't immune to sexual sin. Paul's first letter to the Corinthians addresses situations that even the raciest soaps wouldn't touch. He scolds a man for living with his father's wife, and he chastens the church for putting up with the situation, which even pagan cultures would have considered terribly wrong. In Paul's second letter to the Corinthians, we find that the man repented and was restored.

Sexual desires are incredibly powerful, and if they aren't understood, they can lead to tragic consequences. If we give in to our lusts, we harm everyone involved. On the other hand, if we simply repress our desires, we become sullen and angry, and eventually, we feel compelled to satisfy those desires somehow, someway, with someone. The Scriptures tell us boldly that sex is one of the most beautiful gifts God has given us. We need to think rightly about it so we can enjoy it, but even when we fail, God is there to redeem and restore us.

> The hunger for love is much more difficult
> to remove than the hunger for bread.
> MOTHER TERESA

========================= Fresh Insights =========================

What does sex mean to you? If we are honest, to some of us, sex means love, and for others, sex is a way to control men. Women who were sexually abused or abandoned sometimes conclude that real relationships aren't possible. They believe they can never enjoy rich, warm, authentic love, so they settle for a second best option. If these women are married, they get confused about what a relationship with their husbands can be. They may use sex as a reward or punishment or tool to manipulate their husbands to give them something they want. Sooner or later, however, this unwritten contract breaks down. Both feel used, anger flares, and the relationship crumbles.

Unfortunately, the path away from pure sex is about selfishness. When we open our eyes to take a long look at the ways we think and act sexually, we soon realize that cultural images and messages strongly influence us. Virtually every beauty product promises that it will make us more sexually attractive and sensuous. Television programs and movies that would have been considered scandalous only a few years ago are now standard fare all day and all night. Sitcoms, dramas, and soaps graphically depict the delights of illicit sex (very seldom do they show sexual delights in marriage) but with very few negative consequences. If there are consequences, they fit into more drama and sex later, or the pain is quickly resolved. This barrage of messages makes sex apart from marriage seem entirely normal and even desirable!

For a reality check, all we have to do is talk to friends whose lives and families have been torn apart by sexual indiscretion. The heartache doesn't resolve before the last commercial. Instead, it lasts for years and stains every relationship. Yes, God graciously forgives, but the laws of nature don't exempt us from the consequences of our choices.

Why are so many women's hearts consumed by sexual issues, such as guilt over past indiscretions, lust for sexual encounters today, or elaborate attempts to keep their current sexual sins from being exposed? The answer goes back to the first paragraphs of this chapter: God has made us sexual beings, and we long to find joy and thrills with the one we love. The drive to fulfill our longings sparks our creativity in the bedroom, but it also makes us vulnerable to temptations. In Proverbs, Solomon often describes the cause-and-effect relationship of our choices. In the first nine chapters, he focuses on sex, and he vividly depicts the unfolding of sexual temptation and sin. One passage shows how a seductive woman patiently weaves her web to lure a prospective lover, but it could just as easily be about a man tempting a woman to have sex with him. The images Solomon paints could be the script for an episode of *Desperate Housewives*. Take a look:

> While I was at the window of my house, looking through the curtain, I saw some naive young men, and one in particular who lacked common sense. He was crossing the street near the house of an immoral woman, strolling down the path by her house. It was at twilight, in the evening, as deep darkness fell. The woman approached him, seductively dressed and sly of heart. She was the brash, rebellious type, never content to stay at home. She is often in the streets and markets, soliciting at every corner. She threw her arms around him and kissed him, and with a brazen

look she said, "I've just made my peace offerings and fulfilled my vows. You're the one I was looking for! I came
out to find you, and here you are! My bed is spread with
beautiful blankets, with colored sheets of Egyptian linen.
I've perfumed my bed with myrrh, aloes, and cinnamon.
Come, let's drink our fill of love until morning. Let's enjoy
each other's caresses, for my husband is not home. He's
away on a long trip. He has taken a wallet full of money
with him and won't return until later this month." So she
seduced him with her pretty speech and enticed him with
her flattery. (Proverbs 7:6-21 NLT).

And how did the man respond to her invitation? Solomon tells
us, "He followed her at once, like an ox going to the slaughter. He
was like a stag caught in a trap, awaiting the arrow that would pierce
its heart. He was like a bird flying into a snare, little knowing it
would cost him his life" (Proverbs 7:22-24 NLT).

No woman consciously and rationally decides to ruin her life
by committing sexual sin, but far too many of us play with the
thought and then take tiny steps. Each step makes the next one
easier, and eventually we plunge headlong into disaster. The process
often begins with seemingly harmless fantasies.

Women sometimes tell me, "Oh, Julie, my sexual fantasies are
no big deal. And to be honest, they're the only part of my day I
really enjoy." Thinking and planning great sexual experiences with
our husbands is good and right, but fantasies about sexual indiscretions *are* a big deal. They consume our thoughts, shape our hearts,
and blind our eyes so that we can't see God's good purposes. Quite
often, fantasies are the initial fuel that propels us toward devastating
sin. Gradually, inconceivable behavior becomes thinkable and then
attractive. Finally, we toy with a plan of action. These thoughts may
seem harmless and innocent at first, but they eventually show their
destructive power—if not in actual sinful behavior, at least in stealing
our joy, distorting our expectations, and poisoning our relationships.
No wonder Jesus revealed the true nature of lustful thoughts.

Society drives people crazy with
lust and calls it advertising.

JOHN LAHR

Cultivating Selfless Sex

We need spiritual perception to look beneath the thrills or heart-aches of our sex lives to uncover our deepest motives in relation-ships. When we can extend love and receive love in a committed relationship in marriage, we have a firm foundation for the crucial elements of great sex: communication and creativity.

To fully give and receive love in a committed marriage, under-standing one another and being able to create intimate moments together is crucial, especially if past hurts are robbing your joy in the bedroom. But you don't have to worry; I am not going to ask you to sing "Amazing Grace" three times before you jump in bed with your man. But I do believe that some relationship principles can make your love sweeter than honey.

First, communication and creativity take time. African writer Ernes-tine Banyolak beautifully illustrates the concept of lovemaking.

> A man's experience is like a fire of dry leaves. It is easily kindled, flaring up suddenly and dying down just as quickly. A woman's experience on the other hand is like a fire glow-ing charcoal. Her husband has to tend to these coals with loving patience. Once the blaze is burning brightly, it will keep on glowing and radiating warmth for a long time.

Take time for love and each other.

Second, once you make the time, you have to communicate. Great lovers are able to share meaningful parts of their lives with the one they love—even the barriers that are preventing passionate sex in the bedroom. Good sex is the fruit of caring for, accepting, and valuing your love before, during, and after lovemaking. Most women I have talked to about their poor sex lives with their hus-bands say they have lost their pillow talk.

Third, most couples have lost the art of touch. Secure lovers are able to participate in meaningful nonsexual touch: back rubs, holding hands, a gentle kiss, holding each other, a stroke of the hair…Such meaningful touch can lead to emotional, relational, and physical bonding. Physical closeness can promote relational closeness and enhance intimacy. A woman recently told me, "He doesn't even know what I like—how I like to be touched anymore." Most sex therapy programs stop the sex and teach couples to start with nonsexual touch all over again. Makes sense, doesn't it? No wonder we have lost creativity.

Finally, couples who enjoy fulfilling sexual lives develop the art of being creative together. But this doesn't come without tenderness. Noted author Ingrid Trobisch says, "The greatest erogenous zone in a woman's body is her heart." Sex was never meant to be a single act of expression or feeling. On the contrary, gentleness, acts of kindness, and self-sacrifice—you know, those little words that fit into the word *love*—all combine to become the building blocks of sexual satisfaction. Sex is about joining with your partner as God designed for warmth, intimacy, and bonding. Allow the creative acts of sex to enhance the fun, laughter, and excitement of true intimacy together. (See Proverbs 5:15-19; Song of Songs 7:10-13; 1 Corinthians 7:3-5; Hebrews 13:4.)

Steps Forward

I hope my observations help you to understand a little more about God's intent for sex and to reconsider your own perspective. Our desire for meaningful, thrilling sex in marriage isn't warped; that's what God wants us to enjoy. Marriage provides the safety and security we need in order to give ourselves—body, mind, and soul—to the one we love.

If you're suffering from guilt, repressed desires, or uncontrollable fantasies, find a friend or counselor who can help you sort out the confusing messages in your mind. Don't remain isolated and try to figure it out alone. That seldom works. Thank God for the desires he has put in you. Don't repress them, but don't let them control your life either. Your ability to say no to an illicit relationship is a testimony to your love and intimacy with God.

When you feel comfortable enough to bring up the topic with your husband, take the initiative to talk to him about your sex life. He may feel just as awkward as you do, but open and honest conversations about sex are just as important as communication about finances, children, in-laws, and every other significant part of your relationship. If you need help sorting out what you want, what he wants, and how you can take steps forward to find sexual fulfillment, check out some helpful Christian websites and books.[6]

Be careful about what you read and what you watch on television and at the movies. Our minds aren't in neutral as these images enter our brains. The messages powerfully shape our expectations, hopes, and dreams. In an earlier chapter, we looked at Paul's encouragement to choose to think about things that are good, noble, right, lovely, and pure. This passage (Philippians 4:8-9) applies in every area of our lives and none more than our sexual thoughts. For substantive change to occur in our hearts, many of us need to make drastic changes in the way we handle our TV remotes. Instead of watching sex-filled sitcoms and dramas, watch something far healthier, read a book, or better yet, enjoy sexual intimacy with your husband. For inspiration, read Song of Songs in a modern translation, and let its poetry and symbolism enflame your passions.

I've talked to many women who feel deeply disappointed because their husbands aren't as romantic as they'd like them to be. I understand. I love Tim with all my heart, but sometimes...well, you understand. I encourage women not to sit back and complain that Lancelot has turned into Homer Simpson. Instead, take initiative to create romantic moments that build up your love for each other and that stimulate him sexually (it usually doesn't take much).

I hope you'll bring God into your bedroom. Is that a strange concept for you? For many women, it's revolutionary. Adam and

Eve enjoyed sex, naked and unashamed, in full sight of God in the Garden. They didn't think of hiding from God because they recognized that all parts of life (including sex) are good gifts from a wise and kind Creator. When we think about sex, God is right there with us. When we plan a romantic evening, God delights in our pursuits. And when we experience the thrill of intimacy, romance, and love with our husbands, God smiles. Remembering that he is with us all day every day can help us shape our thoughts to fit his purposes. Our guilt dissolves in his mercy and grace, and we live every moment in the light of his goodness.

Women who struggle with lustful fantasies are like everyone else—they long to be loved. They think they can fill the holes in their hearts by seducing men. They may succeed in the immediate goal but still fail miserably in the long-term goal. When sex isn't coupled with authentic, committed love, women soon feel used and discarded. The thrill of the chase and the act of forbidden sex are initially exhilarating, but they aren't worth the price. With God's care, women today can experience forgiveness, healing, and love just as the woman at the well and the adulteress did. Women who fantasize about sexual liaisons can know that God's way is best, and they can trust him. For some, sexual fulfillment can be elusive. Whether it takes a lot of effort or very little, a long time or an instant, we can see this part of our lives far more clearly when we adopt God's perspective on sexuality.

Have you been looking in the mirror in this chapter, or have you been thinking of a friend who is using her body to find love or power through sex? Hormones and urges are incredibly powerful, but God's Spirit, God's power, and God's gift of a trusted friend can help anyone find peace.

Start today by confessing your sinful lust to God, repenting, and asking God to fulfill the longing in your heart for love and affirmation with positive lusting after him...and your husband.

Healing the Damage

1. How would you describe lust? What genuine need is it attempting to meet? If you have known of women who gave in to their inordinate lust, what were the results?

2. Read Song of Songs 2:16-17 and 4:3-7. What metaphors do these passages use to describe sexual experiences, and what do those metaphors mean? How might you communicate similar messages to your husband in your own words?

3. Glance again at this chapter's stories of God redeeming people from sexual sin. Which of these stand out to you? Explain your answer.

4. What does sex mean to you? What do you want it to mean to you? Do you struggle with fantasies? If so, how do they affect you?

5. How well do you and your husband communicate about sex? What are some steps you can take toward communication and creativity in the bedroom?

6. What does "bringing God into the bedroom" mean to you? How might you and your husband do that?

Bible Passages on Lust

"It is God's will that you should be sanctified: that you should avoid sexual immorality; that each of you should learn to control his own body in a way that is holy and honorable, not in passionate lust like the heathen, who do not know God; and that in this matter no one should wrong his brother or take advantage of him. The Lord will punish men for all such sins, as we have already told you and warned you. For God did not call us to be impure, but to live a holy life" (1 Thessalonians 4:3-7).

"These are the words of the Son of God, whose eyes are like blazing fire and whose feet are like burnished bronze. I know your deeds, your love and faith, your service and perseverance, and that you are now doing more than you did at first. Nevertheless, I have this against you: You tolerate that woman Jezebel, who calls herself a prophetess. By her teaching she misleads my servants into sexual immorality and the eating of food sacrificed to idols. I have given her time to repent of her immorality, but she is unwilling. So I will cast her on a bed of suffering, and I will make those who commit adultery with her suffer intensely, unless they repent of her ways. I will strike her children dead. Then all the churches will know that I am he who searches hearts and minds, and I will repay each of you according to your deeds" (Revelation 2:18-23).

"I tell you that anyone who looks at a woman lustfully has already committed adultery with her in his heart" (Matthew 5:28).

"Do you not know that your bodies are members of Christ himself? Shall I then take the members of Christ and unite them with a prostitute? Never!...Flee from sexual immorality. All other sins a man commits are outside his body, but he who sins sexually sins against his own body" (1 Corinthians 6:15,18).

"Blessed is the man who perseveres under trial, because when he has stood the test, he will receive the crown of life that God has promised to those who love him.

"When tempted, no one should say, 'God is tempting me.' For God cannot be tempted by evil, nor does he tempt anyone; but each one is tempted when, by his own evil desire, he is dragged away and enticed. Then, after desire has conceived, it gives birth to sin; and sin, when it is full-grown, gives birth to death" (James 1:12-15).

Envy and Jealousy

I love shoes. I usually notice a woman's shoes before I take in much else about her. My feet get jealous quickly if I see a pair of shoes that seem a little nicer or more comfortable than mine.

Do you remember Wanda Holloway, the "Texas cheerleader-murdering mom"? She was sentenced to 10 years in prison for plotting to have the mother of her daughter's cheerleader rival murdered.

Do you remember when, at a practice for the 1994 U.S. figure skating championships, Nancy Kerrigan was attacked with a crowbar to the knee? Kerrigan's competitor, Tonya Harding; Harding's ex-husband, Jeff Gillooly; and her bodyguard, Shawn Eckhardt, hired Shane Stant to injure Kerrigan so she couldn't compete.

Have you heard of Peter Kowalczyk, a contestant on the British show *X Factor*? When Kowalczyk didn't win the competition, he was so jealous that he punched former winner Leona Lewis in the head at a book signing in late 2009.

Have you ever shared good news with people, but their facial expressions said anything but "I'm happy for you"? Their initial look of surprise may have quickly changed to a glint of desire: *You have something I want!* And that hard-edged desire can just as quickly transform into anger. These people's faces scream out their envy and jealousy. Their self-absorbed perceptions cloud their vision and steal their joy. I wish these situations were rare, but they're not.

According to Mr. Webster, envy is "painful or resentful awareness of an advantage enjoyed by another joined with a desire to possess the same advantage." Jealousy is "intolerance of rivalry or unfaithfulness." We often use these terms interchangeably, but there's a distinct difference. According to the *Stanford Encyclopedia of Philosophy*, jealousy involves three people: the subject, the rival, and the beloved, with the focus of attention on the beloved. Envy, however, includes only two people: the subject and her rival, with the focus of attention, of course, on the rival.

What makes women feel envious or jealous?

How about who has the nicest house or car or husband or legs; the biggest bosom, tightest buns, or ripped stomach; the most money or best job or most exciting opportunities? I'm sure you can add to the list.

In a study of 278 employees across 200 organizations, researcher Frederick C. Miner Jr. found that more than 75 percent of respondents observed a jealous situation at work.

This may not surprise you at all, but it surprised me. Even more fascinating was Miner's distinction between jealousy and envy. He asked respondents, "If I could give the [jealous] person a similar benefit, would that satisfy him or her?" If the answer was an honest yes, he labeled the emotion as envy. But if the answer was no, he asked another question: "If I could remove the benefit I gave you, would that satisfy him or her?" If the answer was yes, the emotion was considered jealousy. What's the difference? Having what the other person had (such as more days off, a better title, or higher pay) wasn't enough. Instead, the jealous person desired to hurt the person who had something he or she didn't have. This sheds some light on the stories at the beginning of this chapter.

But that's not all! The jealousy and manipulative behavior cause even more problems. Miner found that 72 percent of jealous people in the workplace attempt to divide their coworkers by getting them to align with them and go against the one they are jealous of.

> Although it's natural that people will talk, the data show that these people are doing more than conveying information. For example, in more than one-third of the situations, jealous people try to undermine (spread rumors, act destructively and so on) the coworkers they're jealous of: one-quarter of the time they try to undermine the position of the benefit provider.[1]

Jealousy is a mental cancer that consumes us. At the core of it is a fear that you don't have value. And the more you look to others and compare yourself to them, the more you'll sit back and continue believing the lie that everybody else has more worth than you do. In *The Conspiracy of Fiesco,* Johann Christoph and Friedrich von Schiller stated that "Jealousy is the great exaggerator." It makes you believe that everybody else is dressed better than you, has a better husband than you, has more fun than you, makes more money than you, and has a better job than you.

Also at the core of jealousy is a continual thirst for more and more and more. If this desire is not controlled, it will eventually consume you. It never lets you rest or find contentment.

The Fine Line

Envy is one of the seven deadly sins (Proverbs 6) and destroys both the person and her relationships. But it can also come in a more benign form, disguised as admiration. And here is where we have to be careful.

We've all been blessed by someone singing a beautiful song and then heard another person remark, "I wish I could sing like that." This comment doesn't carry the anger and resentment we find in truly envious people. Jealousy, too, can be constructive. It is right to be jealous when someone tries to destroy a committed relationship. When a husband's eyes wander to other women, a loving wife responds defiantly, "I won't let any other woman come between my husband and me." Her jealous longing for her husband's love is healthy and just. Jealousy can be fierce, for better or for worse.

Our eyes tell all. When we respectfully admire people's talents, our expressions are different than they would be if we were envious and resentful of them. Self-absorbed envy is full of resentment, but admiration is full of hope and joy.

Is it right to honor and praise people for their accomplishments? Absolutely. Respecting those who have acquired earthly blessings is very important. But our focus should be about them, not us.

Destructive envy and jealousy thrive on comparison. We see what others have and immediately think about what we don't have. Today's advertising plays on this. Magazines, television shows, billboards, and websites shout that we simply have to have this or that product to look our best, feel our best, and do our best. The real message is that we have to look, feel, and do better than other women. They are our rivals. As others have said, we women really don't dress for men. We spend hours getting ready so we can measure up to other women. We compare the brightness of our smiles, the shape of our legs, the classiness of our clothes, the size of our breasts, the loyalty of our friends, and every other conceivable aspect of our lives.

In his excellent book *The Call*, Os Guinness observed that people compare themselves to people with similar talents. For instance, a gifted pianist doesn't compare herself to a plumber, but to other talented pianists. People in business don't compare themselves to pianists, but to others who are gaining higher titles, more power, and fatter salaries. And beautiful women compare themselves to other pretty women, always looking for things to feel good about, but almost always finding things that make them feel inferior.

Envy and jealousy are, at their core, based on discontent. To feel superior, we look for anything and everything wrong with those who are potential rivals. We delight in hearing about other people's character flaws, and when we discover only minor ones, we inflate them so they appear to be enormous. To whom do we inflate them? Anyone who will listen. We are critical and judgmental, finding fault with our rivals' smallest flaws and getting a delicious thrill out of gossiping about it.

A mind consumed with comparison is fertile soil for deception. We twist the truth to make us look a little better and to make our rivals a little worse. Our exaggeration feels so right, we don't even notice we are lying in order to promote ourselves. And nowhere has this kind of exaggeration done more damage than in the church, where it spoils a testimony until it stinks worse than egg salad gone bad. *Things are going great in my life because I am doing things right*, we think—especially when our lives are not as great as we want them to be. If our lives really were that great, we wouldn't need to exaggerate the truth.

When our envy of others turns us against them, we have become jealous. We wish we were as righteous or our husbands were as godly or we had as much money, and we begin to gossip about those who seem to have it all. Jealousy promotes gossip. And gossip promotes division. Evil loves to use such behavior to thwart the unity of the Spirit and the glory of God.

It is not love that is blind, but jealousy.
LAWRENCE DURRELL

Finding Fault

Can you imagine the honor of being Moses' sister? Miriam had watched her brother lead the people of Israel out of Egypt, through the Red Sea, and to Sinai, where he came down from the mountain glowing (yes, glowing!) because he had been with God. In all of history, few people have led their people with such power, humility, and integrity, and Miriam had a front-row seat to every moment of it.

But after a while, being the sister of the great man wasn't good enough for Miriam. She watched as God performed countless miracles through Moses, and she eventually became envious of her brother. She pointed out a flaw in Moses' life and allowed it to dominate her perspective. During his years in exile in the desert, Moses had married Zipporah, the daughter of a Cushite priest. Now, decades after the wedding and quite a while after Moses had led the people out of Egypt, Miriam and her other brother, Aaron, despised Moses because of his wife. But they condemned more than his choice of a bride. They openly questioned Moses' authority as God's chosen spokesman. They spread their dissention by innuendo: ""Has the LORD spoken only through Moses?" And they wanted their share of attention. They asked, "Hasn't he also spoken through us?" (Numbers 12:2).

The Scriptures tell us that the Lord heard Miriam and Aaron. We know that God is omnipresent (he is everywhere all the time) and omniscient (he knows everything). But many of us conveniently forget that he's present and listening when we're wanting what others have and finding fault with them. Envy blinds us, riveting our focus on our own self-centered interests, and we demand what we insist should be ours. God called the three siblings to the tent that housed his visible presence, the tabernacle, where he appeared in a cloud and defended Moses:

> Listen to my words:
> When a prophet of the LORD is among you,
>   I reveal myself to him in visions,
>   I speak to him in dreams.
> But this is not true of my servant Moses;
>   he is faithful in all my house.
> With him I speak face to face,
>   clearly and not in riddles;
>   he sees the form of the LORD.
> Why then were you not afraid
>   to speak against my servant Moses? (Numbers 12:6-8).

God was very unhappy with Miriam, and when the cloud disappeared, she found herself standing there as a leper. She was horrified, and she asked her brother Moses, against whom she had tried to lead a rebellion just moments before, to ask God to heal her. Moses, in humble leadership and without an ounce of vengeance, prayed, "O God, please heal her!" But God replied that she would have to experience seven days of disgrace and isolation as consequences for her sin of envy. After the days passed, she entered the community again, but those days surely had a profound impact on her—and on the rest of the people who learned that envy earned God's stern rebuke and harsh consequences.

This story provides us with two immediate reminders. First, inordinate envy (as opposed to admiration) is serious sin. God sees it as rebellion against him, his purposes, and his path for our lives. When we are convinced we can run our lives better than he can, we demand that he dance to our tune, and we no longer worship him and follow wherever he leads. And second, envy inevitably produces disastrous consequences—the very opposite of what we hoped for. We wanted the position of respect, praise, and admiration others achieved, but envy hardens our hearts and makes us like Miriam in her exile—detestable. Instead of drawing people closer to us, our anger and demands push people away, leaving us socially isolated and emotionally empty.

But Miriam's story also teaches us a lesson about redemption. Yes, sin has serious consequences, but God is more than willing to forgive and restore us. Our time of isolation isn't wasted. There, we learn the inestimable value of repentance. Our hard hearts are softened, and we worship the God who leads us with kindness and strength.

Jealousy...is a mental cancer.

B.C. FORBES

Entitlement is the pervasive sense that we deserve better and more than we currently enjoy. In other words, we see people as rivals if they have more than we do, so envy and jealousy flourish. We entertain a gnawing feeling that God has let us down, people have betrayed us, and circumstances have conspired to ruin our lives. We may smile, but our eyes tell a different story. The look on our faces reveals what is at the core of our hearts: We believe we've been dealt a bad hand.

To be sure, all of us face disappointments. I'm not suggesting that we act like Pollyanna or just try to smile through the heartache. The Scriptures invite us to be brutally honest about our pain, but they also give wonderful hope that God is present, he cares, and he can bring good out of the most horrific difficulties. Entitlement is a "glass half empty" perception of life; faith makes possible a "glass half full" outlook. Our disposition becomes self-fulfilling. If we grumble and complain about how we've been wronged, we'll be so unattractive that we invite further relational disappointments. But if we look for God's hand in every event, we become beacons of hope for everyone around us.

Entitlement breeds comparison, and comparison is the fertile soil of envy and jealousy. Some of us spend so much time comparing ourselves and our circumstances to others that we can't imagine any other way to live. It's an ingrained habit. Our minds and hearts are absorbed by thoughts of how we measure up to other people's beauty, popularity, or wealth. We might think that only desperately poor people or abused people compare themselves to those who have a better life, but that's not the case at all. Even the most beautiful and wealthy—and maybe *especially* the most beautiful and wealthy—compare themselves to others. They spend much of their time trying to keep up with the Joneses.

Of all people, Peter should have been the last person to compare himself with others. During Jesus' final dinner with his followers,

Peter insisted that he would remain faithful even if everyone else abandoned him. Did Jesus smile sadly as he said that Peter would fail three times that very night? A few hours later, Peter fulfilled Jesus' prediction by denying he even knew Jesus. Who intimidated Peter into such cowardice? Threatening soldiers? Demanding religious leaders? No. Peter caved in to household servants standing around a fire watching the proceedings. After his third denial, he heard a cock crow, caught Jesus' eye, and suddenly felt awful pangs of shame.

Three days later, Jesus was alive again and talking with the disciples in a closed room, but the conversation must have been bittersweet. Peter was flabbergasted and overjoyed that Jesus was alive, but the resurrection highlighted Peter's faithlessness. His embarrassment and remorse must have been unbearable.

A couple of weeks later, Peter and a few other disciples were back to work as fishermen, and Jesus appeared again. This time, Jesus had a private conversation with Peter and cleared the air. They talked about Peter's sin and his future as a forgiven person. Jesus told him that he would be a leader of the new church, but he would be persecuted for his faith.

Here's the point for us. After his conversation with Jesus, Peter should have been the most relieved human being the world has ever known, but even in these moments of reconciliation and renewed hope, he got caught up in comparison. He looked up, pointed to John, and asked, "What about him?"

Jesus replied, "If I want him to remain alive until I return, what is that to you? You must follow me" (John 21:22). Peter needed to learn that comparison inevitably creates discontent and results in isolation and emotional pain. He must have learned his lesson because he soon became a strong, compassionate leader of the early church (with the help of the Holy Spirit, who empowered him at Pentecost).

Being thankful can be a natural reaction to an act of kindness or beauty, or it can be a determined response we make even when we don't see any obvious reason to give thanks. Many Bible writers encourage us to rejoice or give thanks. At any time and in any situation, we can adjust our perspective and look at life from God's point of view. Gratitude is surely one of the most attractive character qualities a woman can have.

> Envy slays itself by its own arrows.
> ANONYMOUS

―――――――――― Steps Forward ――――――――――

Envy and jealousy can boil up at any time—while watching talented and gorgeous singers and actors, or while greeting women at church with their rich, handsome, and lovingly attentive husbands. In moments like these, our first task is to notice what's going on in our hearts, take our thoughts captive, and choose gratitude. Some of us have never thought about what we think about, but it's time to learn this skill. I recommend journaling as a way to focus our attention and reflect more deeply. When I journal, I write down my thoughts and feelings, and then I look at what I wrote. I'm completely honest, so I don't have to wonder if I'm telling the truth. I take a deep breath and ask questions like these:

> Does this thought line up with the truth, or am I being too negative or too positive?
>
> Are my feelings consuming me?
>
> What do my feelings reveal about my beliefs about God, myself, and my situation?
>
> What wisdom does God's Word offer about this situation?
>
> For what can I give thanks?

This simple practice, coupled with some insights about the true nature of envy, jealousy, comparison, and entitlement, can help us change our thoughts and therefore our lives. It's not a magical or mystical mind-control gimmick. When Paul wrote to the Corinthian Christians, whose tendency to compare themselves with others had created plenty of problems, he talked about thinking biblically as if it were a battle.

> Though we live in the world, we do not wage war as the world does. The weapons we fight with are not the weapons of the world. On the contrary, they have divine power to demolish strongholds. We demolish arguments and every pretension that sets itself up against the knowledge of God, and we take captive every thought to make it obedient to Christ (2 Corinthians 10:3-5).

In this chapter, we have identified some of these strongholds in our minds. We don't overcome them instantly or with halfhearted efforts, but by laying siege to them—slowly and steadily building our defenses and weaponry, breaking down deceptions, and replacing those lies with God's marvelous truth. If we think about God's truth long enough, it becomes part of our memories so we can recall it instantly. Then, instead of letting our minds drift into unhealthy comparisons and destructive envy, we replace those thoughts with concepts of beauty, truth, love, trust, and gratitude.

At its heart, overcoming envy and jealousy is trusting God with our past, our present, and our future. Instead of clinging to our own thoughts of what will make us happy and demanding that God and others comply with our demands, we open our hands, reach out to God, and trust him to give us true meaning in life. In this way, we "lose our lives," which is the only way to really find them (Matthew 10:39). We don't look at people as competitors or see situations as opportunities to move up the ladder of popularity or prestige. Slowly, powerfully, we become women whose lives are characterized by a deep sense of contentment. We're thrilled with

God's grace toward us, and we realize that his grace has given us far more than we deserve. In a sense, gratitude is the inverse of entitlement, giving thanks instead of demanding, enjoying contentment instead of grumbling, and loving people instead of insisting that they jump through hoops for us.

A thankful heart is a beautiful thing in anyone's life, and it shows up in our expressions as true joy. Do you see this in others? I do, and I love being around those women. Some of them have gotten to this point by dealing with a lifetime of bitter jealousy and overcoming it with God's help. Others learned at an early age that "happiness isn't having what you want; it's wanting what you have." I love that!

Learning to be thankful is a choice, but it's also a process. Don't be discouraged if you find your mind drifting toward comparison and its ugly stepsisters, envy and jealousy. We live in a world soaked in discontent, and it takes a lot of wisdom and courage to see real change in our perceptions. But it can happen! Feed your soul with good messages from God's Word and from the encouragement of trusted friends who are on the same journey. Be honest with each other, and form a pact of sisters who are committed to be women of authentic gratitude. Your choice to be thankful will make amazing changes in the way you process life.

God gave you a gift of 86,400 seconds today.
Have you used one to say thank you?
WILLIAM A. WARD

Healing the Damage

1. Compare and contrast envy and jealousy.

2. What are some ways envy and jealousy thrive on comparison?

3. In what areas of life do women compare themselves to others? How do these comparisons affect them, their outlook, and their relationships?

4. Do you journal? If so, how does journaling help you identify and change the way you think? If you don't, look at the questions about journaling in this chapter. How might this practice help you?

5. Read 2 Corinthians 10:3-5. In what way is correcting our thinking like warfare? What does it mean to take our thoughts captive to the obedience of Christ? How can we do that?

6. What are some ways you can cultivate gratitude in your heart?

7. Take some time to write God a note to thank him for his grace, for those you love, and for what you're learning.

Bible Passages on Envy and Jealousy

"A tranquil heart gives life to the flesh,
but envy makes the bones rot" (Proverbs 14:30 ESV).

"Let us walk properly as in the daytime, not in orgies and drunkenness, not in sexual immorality and sensuality, not in quarreling and jealousy" (Romans 13:13 ESV).

"Love is patient and kind; love does not envy or boast" (1 Corinthians 13:4 ESV).

"If you have bitter jealousy and selfish ambition in your heart, do not be arrogant and so lie against the truth. This wisdom is not that which comes down from above, but is earthly, natural, demonic. For where jealousy and selfish ambition exist, there is disorder and every evil thing" (James 3:14-16 NKJV).

"Therefore, [put] aside all malice and all deceit and hypocrisy and envy and all slander" (1 Peter 2:1 NKJV).

"You are still fleshly. For since there is jealousy and strife among you, are you not fleshly, and are you not walking like mere men?" (1 Corinthians 3:3 NKJV).

7

$\mathcal{N}$eed for $\mathcal{C}$ontrol

We may not be able to control all that happens to
us, but we can control what happens inside us.

BENJAMIN FRANKLIN

I love seeing a woman who is in control—she's confident, put
together, and organized. When my makeup goes on right,
my hair actually obeys, and my coffee doesn't manage to find its
way onto my shirt before Zach and I get out the door for school,
it's a good day. *Maybe.*

Leave it to PMS, a long line at the pharmacy, a fender bender
in morning traffic, and being late for my dentist appointment to
awaken the bear within me—the inner drive to control.

Have you been on your way to meet a girlfriend for lunch, only
to bump into a few frustrating mishaps on the way and finally
arrive to find out your order is all wrong? It's easy to want to scream,
scratch someone (in Jesus' name), or just run.

I'm often amazed to see how quickly and easily a well-planned
day can nose-dive into hopeless disarray. When things get out of
control, I want to jump in and take control and straighten everyone and everything out.

But the compulsive need to "direct, dominate, and command"
(the definition of *control* in one dictionary) can be destructive. Especially when you can do absolutely nothing to change things!

Straining to control everything is like trying to catch the wind.

We can't do it! We sense this intuitively, and we understand that giving in to the "control freak" within us goes directly against the biblical command to "trust in the LORD with all your heart and lean not on your own understanding" (Proverbs 3:5). God already knows what we need, and come to think of it, he surely can run our lives much better than we ever could. And yet, calming the "control monster" within is difficult.

Overcoming our drive for personal control may be the greatest challenge we face in our spiritual development and our quest for a deeper, more intimate relationship with Jesus Christ. This universal struggle to control our lives and especially our relationships is particularly prevalent among women. When Eve ate from the tree of the knowledge of good and evil in the Garden of Eden, God told her, "Your desire will be for your husband, and he will rule over you" (Genesis 3:16). The Hebrew word translated *desire* means "to compel, to urge, to seek control." The New English Translation reads, "You will want to control your husband." (Tim just said amen.)

A lackadaisical attitude of just letting go surely can't please God, for he is a God of order. But micromanaging and trying to control every situation and every person in our lives is not only stressful, it's wrong. God doesn't need us to control everything. He wants us to submit our wills to him. That not only pleases him but makes us wonderfully secure.

Insecure women feel out of control, and that is terrifying to them. They may use various tactics to make sense of their lives and achieve some semblance of stability. Some try to gain control over their friends and family by doing everything they can to please them and make them happy. Other people control situations by pushing people away, and still others feel compelled to intimidate and dominate those around them in order to feel better about themselves.

The attempt to dominate and control others is usually rooted in emotional insecurity and should never be confused with love. Some of us have been the victims of domineering people. Even the desire to fix other people's problems—which, to be sure, is meant to look like the height of selfless compassion—is often a masked attempt to control others to make us feel more significant. Our service, then, is about us, not them. People who are deeply hurt often are the most demanding, controlling people in the world.

We are often surprised when we see the control monster in hardened addicts or psychopaths, but we don't expect to see it in our churches or when we look in the mirror. Too often, I've heard stories of conflict between women who claim to follow the Lord. Their tension may have started with a simple disagreement, but soon, neither woman is willing to lose or even compromise, and the monster of control takes over, tearing the friendship to shreds. By then, the initial issue has long vanished, and the chief concern is winning the battle. The fruit of the Spirit gives way to the fruit of the flesh, and each woman tries to figure out a way to destroy the other.

The fight is particularly nasty in Christian circles, where women feel compelled to appear gentle and loving. When these women turn against each other, they smile as they stab their knives of gossip into each other's hearts. When someone has the gall to confront either of them, the combatant glares, "She deserves it."

The Root of the Evil

Someone defined evil as "doing something wrong and feeling good about it." Some definitions are far more elaborate and erudite, but none are more insightful. At its heart, evil says, "I want what I want when I want it, regardless of what I have to do to get it or who gets hurt." When we think of evil, our minds quickly jump to mass murderers like Hitler or Stalin, or to serial killers like Jeffrey Dahmer. But women have had their day in the darkness too. The names of Karla Homolka, Rosemary West, and Marybeth Tinning don't roll off our tongues, but these women butchered dozens of people, and Mao Tse-tung's wife, Jiang Qing, led her country into the cultural revolution that ultimately killed more than 500,000 people.

Evil, though, isn't in just "those people." The propensity to consider

only our own desires resides in each of us, waiting to be enflamed
to dominate those around us. In our lives, it surfaces in selfishness
and the desire to control people instead of loving them. From the
time Adam and Eve sinned in the Garden, a war has raged in our
hearts. The prophet Jeremiah observed, "The heart is deceitful above
all things and beyond cure. Who can understand it?" (Jeremiah
17:9). God has gloriously redeemed us, but vestiges of our old, sinful nature remain in us until our transformation is complete when
we see Jesus face-to-face. The compulsion to control people, then,
is in all of us. We carry seeds of this desire in our hearts, and they
germinate and sprout when we demand our own way, intimidate
others, and control those we claim to love.

In our years of marriage, I have learned the hard way the difference between controlling and loving Tim. Patience doesn't run in
my genes, and I can get easily frustrated with clothes on the floor,
toothpaste in the sink, and the toilet seat left up (again!). Honestly,
my natural reaction is to make sure Tim knows how irritated I
am, which easily turns into nagging, conniving, and saying things
like "If you don't _____, I will _____!" But when I try to control
Tim, we just get mad at each other, and I destroy the intimacy we
ultimately both want. Maybe you've been there too. I'm learning
that controlling and loving can't coexist, because true, godly love
is sacrificial.

Jezebel's Means to a Selfish End

In the entire scope of the Bible, perhaps no woman is as well
known for her conniving wickedness as King Ahab's wife, Jezebel.
In fact, her name has become synonymous with evil. At one point,
Ahab noticed a particularly beautiful vineyard owned by a man
named Naboth. Ahab offered to buy the land or give Naboth another vineyard in exchange, but Naboth wanted to keep the land his
fathers had tilled for generations. Ahab went home "sullen and
angry" because Naboth had turned him down.

Jezebel, though, wasn't a woman to take no for an answer, and she had no patience for a pouting husband. She promised to get the vineyard for Ahab and concocted a plan. She secretly wrote letters to the elders of the city where Naboth lived, signed Ahab's name, and put his royal seal on them. The letters read, "Proclaim a day of fasting and seat Naboth in a prominent place among the people. But seat two scoundrels opposite him and have them testify that he has cursed both God and the king. Then take him out and stone him to death" (1 Kings 21:9-10).

The elders undoubtedly knew the reputations of Ahab and Jezebel, so they felt they had no option but to comply. They followed the instructions to the letter and reported back to Jezebel that Naboth was dead. She immediately took possession of the vineyard and gave it to Ahab.

Jezebel may have thought she pulled off a covert operation, but God knew the truth of her wicked conspiracy. He sent Elijah to confront the royal couple. His judgment was as harsh as their selfishness had been cruel. Elijah told Ahab, "I have found you...because you have sold yourself to do evil in the eyes of the LORD" (1 Kings 21:20). And he related God's message to the king: "I am going to bring disaster on you. I will consume your descendants and cut off from Ahab every last male in Israel—slave or free. I will make your house like that of Jeroboam son of Nebat and that of Baasha son of Ahijah [who experienced God's ultimate punishment], because you have provoked me to anger and have caused Israel to sin" (1 Kings 21:21-22).

Elijah continued, proclaiming God's message of judgment for Jezebel: "Dogs will devour Jezebel by the wall of Jezreel" (1 Kings 21:23). The historian tells us that God judged Ahab and Jezebel for more than this one conspiracy. "There was never a man like Ahab, who sold himself to do evil in the eyes of the LORD, urged on by Jezebel his wife. He behaved in the vilest manner by going after idols, like the Amorites the LORD drove out before Israel" (1 Kings

21:25). God didn't strike them that day, but we find the rest of the story in 2 Kings 9. Jezebel experienced the gruesome death that God planned for her and that spoke volumes about the Lord's attitude toward wickedness.

When we read the Old Testament stories, we may feel repulsed by the harsh punishment God inflicts on those who choose sin over righteousness. Some of us even think that the two parts of the Bible, the Old and New Testaments, give very different images of God: harsh in the Old and full of grace in the New. But that's not the case at all. The Old Testament contains some of the most beautiful stories of God's amazing love in the Scriptures. In fact, that part of the Bible has more references to God's love than the New Testament. Certainly, we find the culmination of God's grace in Jesus, but the entire Old Testament points to the Messiah, who would come to pay for our sins. And in the New Testament, we find the certainty of God's righteous judgment (never capricious, but always just) to respect the wishes of those who choose selfishness and sin over his offer of redemption.

The judgment we read about in Revelation and other New Testament books is similar to the justice we read about earlier in the Bible. The Scriptures are a seamless story of the promise of a Redeemer, our desperate need for a Savior, and God's willingness to respect our choices to follow him or not. Grace and judgment are found throughout the Bible.

The story of Jezebel teaches us a valuable and simple lesson: There are consequences to our selfish choices. Some of us experience consequences immediately when people recoil at our demands and our attempts to control them. We may lose friends and find ourselves alone. But many times, we may not suffer the consequences of our selfishness until later—perhaps not until we see Jesus. At that time, if we're believers, our selfish attitudes and actions will be burned up, and to some degree at least, we'll forfeit the joy of hearing God say, "Well done, good and faithful servant." Control masks itself in many different ways, but even well-intended attempts to make everything okay for everyone will only leave us frustrated. *We are not God.* And I don't know about you, but trying to control myself is a big enough task—one that I can't do without Jesus' help. I think I'll leave controlling others to him.

> He who controls others may be powerful,
> but he who has mastered himself is mightier still.
>
> TAO TE CHING

Fresh Insights

Our reflections on the evil of being demanding and controlling aren't pleasant, are they? Maybe you were tempted to put this book down and walk away while reading this chapter. Let's face it: Getting what we want feels good, but control freaks aren't fun to be around. We're all selfish at heart, and the monster of control can't be mastered without the grace and strength of the Holy Spirit. God wants us to be honest about our thoughts, attitudes, and actions so we can experience his amazing, cleansing love in the depths of our hearts. The compulsion to control thrives in hidden places, so the best thing we can do is to bring it into God's light. Paul tells us that at our core, all of us are sinful people. In a long and brutal depiction of the human heart, Paul reminds the Roman Christians, "All have turned away, they have together become worthless; there is no one who does good, not even one" (Romans 3:12).

Even as redeemed believers, we still struggle with our sinful desires, and sometimes they threaten to overwhelm us. In the same letter, Paul reflected on the conflict in his own heart: "I do not understand what I do. For what I want to do I do not do, but what I hate I do...For what I do is not the good I want to do; no, the evil I do not want to do—this I keep on doing" (Romans 7:15,19). Paul loudly and clearly proclaims the solution to his dilemma in the next chapter: God's forgiveness. There is no condemnation for God's children, but that's no excuse to keep deliberately sinning. Therefore daily I have to reckon myself dead to sin and alive to God, offering my life to him.

When we think we've arrived spiritually or that we've become immune to the possibility that sin will surface in our lives, we're vulnerable to stumble and fall. The fact that we've been deeply hurt or that we've acted a certain way all our lives is no excuse. All of us, from the newest believer to the most mature saint, need to be aware of the internal struggle between our selfish natures and God's Spirit. Paul wrote about this conflict in his letter to the Galatians: "So I say, live by the Spirit, and you will not gratify the desires of the sinful nature. For the sinful nature desires what is contrary to the Spirit, and the Spirit what is contrary to the sinful nature. They are in conflict with each other, so that you do not do what you want" (Galatians 5:16-17).

The problem is that we often fail to label the desires of our sinful nature as sin. Instead, we justify our anger, excuse our selfishness, rationalize our demands, minimize the damage our evil has on others, and deny we're wrong at all. However, hurting other people is never right, regardless of how poorly they treat us. If we aren't honest about our sin, we won't be able to trust God for his forgiveness, cleansing, and transformation.

You may be thinking, *But Julie, you don't understand. I was terribly hurt by my parents* [or spouse or friends or boss or children or someone else]. *I need to control people around me so no one can hurt me again.* I understand. Protecting yourself this way would make perfect sense—if God had not provided a way for us to experience healing and hope. Taking a look into our background gives us insight about the hurt, fear, and anger that cloud our eyes and distort every relationship in our lives, but even an accurate understanding offers only an incomplete answer to the problem.

Controlling and manipulating other people in order to protect ourselves is no real way to live. Women who function this way can never experience the beauty and intimacy of relationships that God intended. We can't magically make ourselves better, but we can ask God to touch us at the depths of our hearts. Our pain isn't too big for him, and our "control monster" isn't too strong for his Spirit to master. Jesus promises to heal the wounds, calm the fears, and restore a sense of joy and purpose to our lives, but we have to submit our wills to him.

Regardless of how badly we've been victimized by other people's evil, our pain doesn't excuse us when we respond in kind. We have to face the evil in our own lives and then make choices to deal with both the deep hurts that propel us to control others and the daily opportunities to love people instead of demanding that they comply with our wishes. Next time you switch into "control" mode, remember that you're dealing with one of God's children—a man or woman whom you are commanded to love, not manipulate.

> The one thing over which you have absolute
> control is your own thoughts.
> PAUL THOMAS

Steps Forward

The first step to grappling with our own monster of control is to admit that we have a problem—confessing our manipulative nature as a sin that destroys relationships with the people we love. Oftentimes, in the moment when we lash out, we forget the hurtful consequences of our actions. All of us have been hurt in some way by the evil of control. But rather than outscheming our archrival and taking revenge, we can take action to experience healing.

Wise, mature friends or counselors can help us begin the process and take bold steps toward wholeness. As we enjoy God's goodness and grace more fully than ever before, we can rest, find peace, and stop compulsively controlling people around us. As we learn to trust God with the people in our lives, we realize how futile our attempts at control really are. And we become free to be the women God created us to be, rather than trying to play God and control everyone else.

Until we meet Jesus face-to-face, we'll experience the wrestling match between the selfish desires inherent in our sinful natures and the Spirit's power and purpose for us. As our eyes are opened to this struggle, we won't be surprised when the Holy Spirit taps us on the shoulder and says, *That was selfish. Don't control her like that.* And we'll learn to respond by repenting and asking for God's help rather than persisting in the controlling habits that destroy our relationships.

The thirst to have our own way is central to human nature, but it is an enemy of a life of faith. Jesus repeatedly taught us to live another way: to stop demanding and start giving thanks, and to replace fear-inspired control of others with love, which respects others' decisions. Jesus never controlled people. He spoke the truth and let people decide how they wanted to respond. Some people, like the forgiven woman in Luke 7, poured out their hearts in love for him, but others, like the rich young ruler, walked away from Jesus—and Jesus let those people go.

To overcome evil, Jesus went to the cross. He knew that forgiveness is the only solution to the evil in us and in our relationships with others. The believers in Corinth continued to dabble in evil after they became followers of Christ. Paul wrote them a scathing letter, exposing their sin and encouraging them to repent. Later, he learned that his letter had hit the mark. He then wrote them to affirm their choice to soak up God's forgiveness—a remarkable account of the power of forgiveness.

> Even if I caused you sorrow by my letter, I do not regret it. Though I did regret it—I see that my letter hurt you, but only for a little while—yet now I am happy, not because you were made sorry, but because your sorrow led you to

repentance. For you became sorrowful as God intended and
so were not harmed in any way by us. Godly sorrow brings
repentance that leads to salvation and leaves no regret, but
worldly sorrow brings death. See what this godly sorrow
has produced in you: what earnestness, what eagerness
to clear yourselves, what indignation, what alarm, what
longing, what concern, what readiness to see justice done
(2 Corinthians 7:8-11).

I love his statement that "godly sorrow brings repentance that
leads to salvation and leaves no regret." When we have God's perception about the evil in our lives, we feel genuine sorrow, but not the
kind of remorse that leaves us feeling crushed. Instead, this kind of
sorrow leads us to the foot of the cross, where we come away forgiven,
clean, and full of desire to please God more than ever before.

Of course, the issue of control can cause problems both ways.
You may not be controlling others as much as being controlled by
them. You may be in relationships with people who aren't sorry for
demanding your compliance. Whether they are friends, coworkers, or your spouse, these people relish their power! The good news
is that we don't have to remain victims of their abuse. With some
encouragement, healing, and new skills, we can learn to confront
these controlling people and invite them to build a relationship
based on trust and respect rather than manipulation and control.
If they accept our offer, we can begin with a fresh start, but if not,
we have to protect ourselves.

Trust is the foundation of any genuine relationship, and manipulating other people destroys that trust. Controlling others or letting
ourselves be controlled by others may occasionally seem justified,
but it ruins relationships. God wants each of us to learn self-control
and leave changing others up to him. That means setting healthy
boundaries rather than responding as victims. You are God's precious creation, and no individual has the authority to subject you
to manipulation.

To become wise in difficult relationships, we need God's direction, the advice of mature friends, and a healthy dose of courage to take bold steps forward, or in some cases, to learn to keep our mouths shut. Both are appropriate at different times, but we desperately need God's guidance to figure that out. The book of Proverbs is a great place to start in God's Word; it's jam-packed full of godly counsel about how to develop healthy relationships.

Interacting with other people can be difficult because our sinful nature is naturally selfish and controlling, so we have to counteract that tendency in order to unselfishly care about other people. Only Jesus' power can replace the desire to control with the desire to love.

As we've examined the destructive nature of control in this chapter, whose faces have come to mind? Or have you been looking in the mirror at the selfishness and manipulation in your own eyes? Learn to see this issue from God's point of view. Control is a big deal to God. Other people's lives belong to him, so we shouldn't try to take them into our own hands. Conquering the control monster requires submitting our selfish wills to God. In that place of humility, we can experience his forgiveness, extend forgiveness to others, and be lights for others so they can see the truth about their lives. Rather than backstabbing and manipulating God's precious children, we can learn to love them when we let God control and reform our selfish hearts.

Healing the Damage

1. How would you define evil? What are some examples that come to mind?

2. Do you agree that demanding compliance and trying to control others are common forms of evil in our lives? Explain your answer.

3. What are some ways we deny, excuse, minimize, or justify our desire to control others? What are the benefits of naming control what it really is (sin) instead of dodging it?

4. Our compulsion to control may come from experiences of hurt in our past. How does this information help us? How does hurt paralyze us and keep us locked into patterns of self-protection and compulsive control?

5. Read Galatians 5:16-17. What does this struggle look like in your mind, your heart, and in your actions? In what ways are you winning? In what ways are you losing?

6. Read 2 Corinthians 7:8-11. How would you describe godly sorrow? How is it different from worldly sorrow?

7. As you read this chapter, have any attitudes and actions come to light that need God's forgiveness and healing? If so, take some time now to talk to him about them.

Bible Passages on Control

"Pride goes before destruction,
And a haughty spirit before stumbling.
It is better to be humble in spirit with the lowly
Than to divide the spoil with the proud"
(Proverbs 16:18-19 NASB).

"Commit your way to the LORD,
trust also in Him, and He will do it" (Psalm 37:5 NASB).

"Offer the sacrifices of righteousness,
And trust in the LORD" (Psalm 4:5 NASB).

"Those who know Your name will put their trust in You,
For You, O LORD, have not forsaken those who seek
You" (Psalm 9:10 NASB).

"Trust in the LORD forever,
For in GOD the LORD, we have an everlasting Rock"
(Isaiah 26:4 NASB).

8

Stressed and Exhausted

We are so tired; my heart and I,
of all the things here beneath the sky.
Only one thing would please us best—
endless, unfathomable rest.

ANONYMOUS

Maybe you feel like Brenda. Stuck, bored, empty, and exhausted, she wondered what went wrong. Brenda saw every point of her slide toward physical and emotional collapse, but she always blamed someone else for her troubles. Like countless other women today, Brenda had high hopes that she could be a success in every part of her life: a loving marriage, responsible and happy kids, and an upward career. Of course, she also dreamed that she could maintain the figure she had when she was 23 and avoid wrinkles, but after three children and a few additional years, she gradually gave up on those goals. Still, Brenda was amazingly adept at making life work. She reminded me of a circus juggler—balancing a dozen china plates without letting a single one shatter to pieces.

But the magic doesn't last forever. Soon after the birth of her third child, Brenda's crystal life began to show a few cracks. She told me she was frustrated because her husband, Jim, and their kids wanted more of her time, but she was up for a promotion at work. If she was going to climb the next rung of the corporate ladder, she simply couldn't look disinterested in her job. Maybe later, but not now.

She got the position, and for a while, everything went well. The raise gave her more money to pay for conveniences that made life more pleasant, but soon, frustration crept into her voice again. She told me, "When I'm at home, I can't stop thinking about work. And when I'm at work, I worry about James and the children." With a deep breath she reflected, "I guess that's just the price I have to pay at this point in my life." And nothing changed.

The next time I talked to Brenda, frustration had turned into resentment. She could barely veil her anger at Jim, their children, and her boss. I was waiting for her to erupt at me too! Everyone seemed to be her adversary. I suggested that she take a look at some priorities, but she cut me off. "You don't understand," she insisted.

I didn't see her again for several months, and when we finally met for coffee, I was stunned by her appearance. Brenda's bubbly self was gone. The light in her eyes had vanished. In its place were tired, darkened, bloodshot eyes. I didn't say anything, but my expression must have given away my thoughts.

She responded by telling me, "I haven't been sleeping well. Not well at all."

I listened attentively to her lament of burdens, misunderstandings, and dead ends in her pursuit of change. Her relationship with Jim had soured, her kids were out of control, and her job demanded more and more of her time. "I can't do anything about any of it," she groaned. "I've tried, but nothing works."

A month later, Jim called to tell me that Brenda had gone to the doctor. "Exhaustion is the diagnosis," he said. "I don't know where we go from here."

- Forty-four percent of working moms admit to being preoccupied about work while at home, and one-fourth say they bring home projects at least one day a week.
- Nineteen percent of working moms reported they often or always work weekends.

- In 2007, 20 percent of workers said they would check in with the office while on vacation.

- Stress and burnout can affect your immune system and has been linked to migraines, digestive disorders, skin diseases, high blood pressure, and heart disease. It causes emotional distress as well.[1]

- In 2007, 32 percent of children in married two-parent families had both parents working year round, full-time.[2]

In our crazy world, the pressure and pain of everyday life takes a deep toll on us physically, emotionally, relationally, and spiritually.

Step back and look at the treadmill most of us are on. The pace of life today is much faster than it was only a few decades ago. *Doing* and *going* creep in to every single minute of our existence. Others have said that if the devil can't make you bad, he'll make you busy, and in contemporary Western society, he has largely succeeded. So often, we pile more commitments and responsibilities on our plate than we can reasonably handle, thinking somehow that burning ourselves out for God and everyone around us is somehow admirable. Nothing could be further from the truth.

Incredible advances in technology and communications provide us with quick solutions, and now we're terribly annoyed with anything less. We thought technology would give us more free time, but the opposite has proven true. We live at a frantic pace, spending less time in reflection, leisure, and relationships, and more time glued to the TV, listening to our iPods, or fiddling with the latest gadget. Strangely, we expect to get more done in less time—with more distractions than ever—and we rush from one thing to another, trying to turn a busy life into a full, satisfying one.

When I look back at the last decade or so, I'm amazed at all of the technological conveniences we enjoy today that weren't even a thought in our minds only a few years ago. Laptops, Internet access, cell phones, texting, iPods, satellite radio...and the list goes on! The advances in communication, medicine, and transportation are mind-boggling. But to be honest, we quickly take them for granted. We've come to expect ease, convenience, and instant gratification all day, every day. These time-saving gadgets have saved us time— and have intruded on it as well.

All change, even positive change, causes some stress. Some transitions bring excitement and joy, but some devastate people. Some have a significant impact on our lives, but some have a minimal effect. In a famous study of the impact of change, various events were assigned a numerical Life Change Unit value. To determine the weight of each event, the research team asked people of different social backgrounds to rate the degree of turmoil each event caused. Then, each event was compared to getting married, which was arbitrarily given a score of 50. The research team was surprised to find that people across the spectrum of age, sex, social position, race, culture, and education scored events very similarly.[3]

death of a spouse	100
divorce	73
death of a close family member	63
detention in jail	63
major injury or illness	53
being fired	47
mortgage foreclosure	30
trouble with boss	23
marriage	50
marital reconciliation	45
retirement	45
pregnancy	40
closing a mortgage on a new home	31

son or daughter leaving home	29
outstanding personal achievement	28
start or end of education	26
change in residence	20

These are just a few of the stresses, both positive and negative, that we women experience. People have various capacities for dealing with stress, but when the numbers add up to 50 within six months, people should see this as a flashing amber light, pay attention to the effects of the pressure in their lives, and take steps to effectively manage stress. If someone experiences a total of 75 or more, the flashing light is bright red! People who endure severe levels of stress, especially for a long time, risk the physical, emotional, and spiritual devastation of burnout and its ugly stepsister, despair.

The 2008 "Stress in America" poll by the American Psychological Association found that two-thirds of Americans identify the economy as a significant source of stress in their lives. In addition, almost one-half of Americans report that job stability is a significant cause of stress.[4] Balancing a part-time or full-time job with the extensive responsibilities of raising a family can be emotionally and physically exhausting.

Stress is a part of every woman's life, but sometimes, life hits really hard. When people experience multiple major stressors in rapid succession, the results can be disastrous. When my friend Linda and her family were seriously injured in a major car accident, stress levels skyrocketed. All four people had prolonged hospital stays—each in a different hospital. Everything spun out of control fast.

High stress levels have become normal for most of us. Actually, the problem isn't stress—it's excessively elevated levels of stress. In his book *Margin: Restoring Emotional, Physical, Financial and Time Reserves to Our Overloaded Lives,* physician Richard Swenson observes that moderate levels of stress stimulate creativity and challenge people to accomplish bigger goals. Like the proverbial frog in the kettle, however, our stress level can rise so gradually that we don't even notice. But as it does, we experience the damaging effects of too much pressure. And when excessive levels of stress seem normal, we fail to notice the problem, and then, of course, we fail to make changes. Under intense pressure, every aspect of our lives is affected: Our thinking isn't as clear, we make bad decisions, our patience evaporates, and consequently, stress levels rise even higher. When this happens, we experience physiological symptoms like headaches and stomach problems, our most important relationships suffer, and we become less and less effective, eventually leading to discouragement, depression, and burnout.[5]

Wise women recognize the progressive pattern of excessive stress, and they do something about it. The graph of increasing stress starts with healthy stress of inspiring challenges but often elevates into the nagging but bearable stress of doing a little too much in too little time. Soon, though, difficulties mount and emotional reserves diminish, and the person experiences oppressive stress because life simply isn't working anymore. If the person doesn't make significant changes at that crucial point, she can suffer emotional, physical, and mental collapse, often described as burnout.

Our energy level and outlook reveal the stage of stress we're experiencing. Those who enjoy inspiration and challenges feel wonderfully alive, and they believe they are making a difference. Their lives are full of adventure. As stress builds, however, the light of life gradually goes out, resentment turns into hopelessness, and eventually, they suffer a devastation of heart, mind, body, and soul.

The good news is that we can arrest the slide at any point along the way—the sooner the better.

> True silence is the rest of the mind, and is to the spirit
> what sleep is to the body, nourishment and refreshment.
> WILLIAM PENN

Diligent Martha

Like you, I've heard countless sermons about Mary and Martha. Almost always, pastors praise Mary for choosing to listen to Jesus, and they chide Martha for being preoccupied with dinner preparations. I think that's too simplistic, and actually, I feel a bit defensive about our friend Martha—maybe because I'm a lot like her! Think about the situation. Jesus was the most honored guest to ever visit her home. It was like inviting the president to come over for dinner. Any woman would want to show respect and give attention to detail so the meal would be wonderful for everybody. And besides, Jesus almost certainly wasn't alone. He brought his entire entourage with him! Even a modest meal required significant attention and effort. No one suggested she was trying to show off for her guests. She simply wanted to honor them appropriately.

In Luke's account of the event, Martha was the one who invited Jesus to her home. She was generous and gracious. I imagine Martha initially thought, *I'm so glad Jesus and his men are here. Mary enjoys being with him, and I think I can handle it all by myself.* But after a while, the stresses of getting everything done on time began to gnaw at Martha, and she may have felt abandoned as Mary sat in the other room, listening to Jesus. *Where is Mary? Doesn't she realize I could use a little help? The least she could do is offer to set the table!* Finally, her anger boiled over. She stormed into the room and said to Jesus, "Lord, don't you care that my sister has left me to do the work by myself? Tell her to help me!" (Luke 10:40).

As Martha's stress level rose, her initial joy must have turned to self-pity and resentment at Mary and probably at Jesus too. Jesus didn't bark at Mary to get moving and help her sister. Instead, he looked into Martha's heart and invited her to redirect her priorities. He told her, "Martha, Martha, you are worried and upset about many things, but only one thing is needed. Mary has chosen what is better, and it will not be taken away from her" (Luke 10:41-42).

The lesson I learn from this moment in Martha's life isn't that honoring guests is unimportant, but that we must look at all of life through the lens of God's priorities. Martha began with pure and noble motives to provide a nice meal for Jesus and his followers, but she could have recognized that she couldn't do it alone without experiencing too much stress. She could have asked for Mary's help much earlier, or she could have made a much simpler meal. (Or she could have asked Jesus to produce a feast from a fish and a loaf of bread lying on the counter that day!) Her error may have been that she didn't make corrections as the stress level rose. When she realized Mary wasn't going to help, she could have adjusted her plans. Preparing a simple meal would have allowed her to enjoy Jesus far more—and the Bible wouldn't include his rebuke for all of us to see. (How embarrassing!)

========= Fresh Insights =========

All of us feel rushed from time to time. If it only happens occasionally, it's no big deal. But if the needle on our dials is on "overload" too long, our bodies and our hearts simply can't take the strain. Some of us can endure excessive stress for a long time before we crash, but others of us crater more quickly. We need to step back and take a good, hard look at the factors that create stress. Some of them are organizational and can be remedied by setting priorities and delegating more effectively. Other stresses, however, have deeper roots in our psychological and spiritual perceptions. Let me highlight a few common reasons our lives might be on overload.

Stressed-Out Kids

Many of our stresses are self-inflicted. Far too often, parents cooperate with the culture to instill inordinately high expectations in children, and then they gripe whenever their kids don't meet those expectations instantly and fully.

An annual study of UCLA freshmen shows that adolescents

are obsessed with having more possessions. Three-fourths of those surveyed said it was essential for them to be "well-off financially" so they can buy all the things they want—a figure almost double the survey results from 40 years ago. In a similar poll, the Pew Research Center found that the top goal for 80 percent of 18- to 25-year-olds is to get rich. David Walsh, a psychologist who leads the National Institute on Media and the Family and the author of *No: Why Kids—of All Ages—Need to Hear It and Ways Parents Can Say It,* observes, "Our kids have absorbed the cultural values of more, easy, fast, and fun." His research found that today's parents spend 500 percent more on their kids, even adjusted for inflation, than the parents a generation ago. "A lot of parents have developed an allergic reaction to their kids being unhappy," Walsh notes.[6] Parents have played a major role in creating their kids' self-absorbed demands, but parents can help reverse this trend—at least in the lives of their own children.

Similarly, parents who fail to engage children in meaningful work around the home erode their children's sense of responsibility, creativity, and drive. Consider the life of an average middle-class American kid today. She has far more disposable wealth than most people in the world and more conveniences than royalty in previous eras. She's entertained all day, every day with television, video games, iPod, and Internet sites, and she's connected to her friends at every moment of every day with her cell phone, text messaging, e-mail, and MySpace or Facebook account. She's completely and continually plugged in, rarely turning off the sights and sounds to come to the surface for conversation.

Always On

The pervasive influence of technology has a powerful impact on our capacity to communicate. Linda Stone, formerly of Apple and Microsoft, coined the term *continuous partial attention* to describe the constant distractions of e-mail, instant messaging, cell phones, and other devices. She describes it on her website:

To pay continuous partial attention is to pay partial attention—continuously. It is motivated by a desire to be a live
node on the network. Another way of saying this is that we
want to connect and be connected. We want to effectively
scan for opportunity and optimize for the best opportunities, activities, and contacts, in any given moment. To
be busy, to be connected, is to be alive, to be recognized,
and to matter. We pay continuous partial attention in an
effort not to miss anything. It is an always-on, anywhere,
anytime, anyplace behavior that involves an artificial sense
of constant crisis. We are always in high alert when we pay
continuous partial attention. This artificial sense of constant crisis is more typical of continuous partial attention
than it is of multi-tasking.[7]

Too Much Debt

Many people today suffer from the burden of financial worries.
Excessive spending has led to oppressive consumer debt. The average person owes many thousands of dollars on credit cards, and
many are so far behind they can only pay the interest each month.
In 2002, the Credit Research Center found that people seeking
the help of credit counselors averaged $43,000 in debt, of which
$20,000 was consumer debt and $8,500 was revolving debt.[8] Surely
the numbers are more distressing now. One of the most common
stressors in marriage is conflict over finances. Some of us can't go
to sleep at night because we're afraid we can't pay the monthly bills,
and others compound this worry with anger and blame at a spouse
or kids for irresponsible spending.

Haunted by Guilt

Some of the nagging anxiety we sense today has to do with our
past—the guilt we feel and the pain we've suffered. We've tried
to forget the pain we've experienced and inflicted on others, but
we can't seem to shake free. We've prayed, we've gone to seminars,

and we've read books, but we still see those faces glaring at us in quiet moments when all we want is to be at peace. We are always on alert, defending ourselves against real or imagined dangers. We can never truly relax. We subconsciously try to fill our lives with busyness to keep from thinking about these ghosts from the past, but the memories infuse every moment of our lives.

Too Willing to Help

Some of us face the haunting specter of burnout because we've never learned to say no. God has given us wonderfully giving hearts, but the requests for help never seem to stop. We give and give. Quite often, we feel that we've made a genuine difference in someone's life, and that spark keeps us going for a while. But all of us need the ability to say, "I'm happy to help, but this is as much as I can do." Without boundaries on our service, we can experience compassion fatigue. Our joy vanishes, our spirit sags, and we start to resent those we used to enjoy helping.

Stages and Phases of Life

Some of the stages of life are more difficult than others, but if we don't recognize these periods, we can easily hit overload. Most of us recognize that the years our children are infants and the years they are adolescents are the most demanding times of being a parent. When we move to another city, our entire fabric of relationships is ripped apart, and it takes most of us about three years to weave rich new friendships. Sickness, job changes, and aging parents bring additional stresses into our lives, often quite unexpectedly.

Sleep

Sleep is the most important component of renewing our bodies on a daily basis. It has become an issue in America because of our fast-paced society. We overexert ourselves taking care of our children, husbands, homes, and work, and as a result, we tend to neglect our own bodies, becoming more anxious and stressed.

Without adequate sleep, our minds and bodies don't recover enough to bring our stress levels down.

God designed our bodies with a built-in need for recovery time. Sleep experts tell us we need eight or nine hours of sleep a night to reduce stress and anxiety. If you're having trouble sleeping, you're not alone. A 2005 National Sleep Foundation "Sleep in America" poll revealed that women are more likely than men to have difficulty falling and staying asleep and to experience more daytime sleepiness at least a few nights or days a week.[9]

Before you try sleep medications, try slowing down, disconnecting from the adrenaline rush of life, and intentionally unwinding. Leisurely read the Bible and other books. Avoid spicy food. Cut back on caffeine during the day. Try to get exercise—it will help you sleep better at night. Don't hesitate to go see a doctor or professional counselor. Sleep loss will make you feel crazy.

If you're anxious about your kids, worried about a job, fretting over a relationship, or just keeping yourself awake at night over the small things in life, try finding ways to hand over to God everything you've been carrying for the day (Matthew 6:34). Besides, you can handle only so much anyway. You need a great night's sleep!

Finding Balance

When stress levels rise, we often neglect the things that can bring us back into balance. Health experts tell us that exercise, eating right, and good sleep are essential to physical and emotional health, and that's even more true when we're burdened by anxieties and stretched thin.

In our world of high expectations, we run great risk of burnout. The first step toward freedom is to notice the pressures our fast-paced lives create and the crushing demands that have become second nature to us. If we can't notice them and name them, we'll stay stuck in the same rut, headed toward self-pity, resentment, strained relationships, and potential physical and emotional collapse. But if we can identify these factors in our lives, we can then realize we have choices—and choices offer hope for real change.

Solutions to the problem of emotional and physical exhaustion come in several forms, and each of us has to determine what works best in our situations. When you look in the mirror, what do you see? Does the person looking back look tired? Is she cranky? Like Martha, does she blame others for not doing enough to help? Many women I know would have to say yes to those questions. That doesn't make them evil people—just women whose lives have gotten out of balance.

On a continuum of balance and burnout, where would you put yourself in this season of your life? If you're not aware of and actively fighting against the pressures to be more, have more, please more, and do more, you're probably slipping toward oppressive stress and burnout.

On a deeper level, we need to look at our motivations for being so driven. Some of us thrive on busyness. In fact, we are proud that we rush from one thing to another. Yes, we complain, but to be honest, we wear our busyness as a badge of honor to impress people around us. Others of us thrive on being needed. Our identity is tied up in the fact that we come through to help when others are in need. We see ourselves as indispensable saviors. We feel great when we've come to someone's rescue, and we feel rotten when people don't need us. When we are driven by busyness and our compulsion to fix others' problems, we are like addicts, living on the adrenaline rush we get from bouncing from one thing to the next or from mending broken situations.

Some of us need to analyze our lives and make structural adjustments. We need to cut some things out of our schedules (and stop using busyness as a badge of honor with our friends). We need to say no to a few things, even if it's just for practice! And we need to

establish better priorities, including exercise, nutrition, sleep, relax-
ation, meaningful devotions, time with friends, exposure to the
beauty of nature, and time when we're not plugged in to any elec-
tronic devices. You may be tempted to try to fix your husband and
children before you find balance in your own life, but resist that
temptation. Go ahead—focus on yourself. If you make progress
with your own life, others will notice and be more willing to follow your lead.

Ultimately, an unbalanced life is a spiritual problem. In his first
letter, Peter encouraged his readers to "Cast all your anxiety on [God]
because he cares for you" (1 Peter 5:7), but notice the context of this
verse. Peter reminds us of one of the overarching themes of Scripture: "God opposes the proud but gives grace to the humble" (verse
5). I believe that many of us forget or ignore this bedrock truth far
too often. We try to figure life out on our own with only a passing
thought or a cursory prayer, we chart our own path without considering God's wisdom and ways, and we take steps to accomplish
goals without trusting God's Spirit to work in and through us. I
hate to say it, but we live like practical atheists, saying we believe in
God but living as if he doesn't exist. Ouch! Peter gives good advice:
"Humble yourselves, therefore, under God's mighty hand, that he
may lift you up in due time" (1 Peter 5:6). Spiritual perception, having our eyes open to see God and his purposes for us, is essential if
our bloodshot eyes are going to become clear again.

In Zephaniah 3:17 (NKJV), we gain a glimpse into how God
sees us as His children: "The LORD your God in your midst, the
Mighty One, will save; He will rejoice over you with gladness, He
will quiet you with His love, He will rejoice over you with singing."
These words soothe my spirit and give me hope as I rush through
my days. He quiets me with His love. Sometimes I experience this
in the coolness of the wind against my face, a beautiful sunset, or
the kind word of a complete stranger. But to see God's love, we
have to stop and look! He rejoices over us with gladness and with

singing, even when we have a bad hair day, act unkindly, or receive devastating news.

In the midst of our busy, imperfect days, we sometimes have to fight to remember that resting is biblical. God commands that we rest, and he invites us to rest in him. Listen to the words of Jesus in Matthew 11:28-30: "Come to Me, all you who labor and are heavy laden, and I will give you rest. Take My yoke upon you and learn from Me, for I am gentle and lowly in heart, and you will find rest for your souls. For My yoke is easy and My burden is light." In the midst of your rushed and hectic days, Jesus invites you to come to him, to study about him, and to learn from him about his ways. He will give you rest and a myriad of other beautiful blessings, such as peace (John 14:27), love (Jeremiah 31:3), joy (John 15:11), and ultimately, abundant life (John 10:10). So take your busy schedule to him and ask him to help you fulfill your obligations and prioritize your day.

God's peace and rest is yours for the taking. In his presence, as we recognize his sufficiency, our spirits can be still as we allow him to guide and control our at-times hectic lives. You don't have to do *everything*—that's impossible. All you have to do each day is obey God. Do what he wants, and you may find that some of the other things on your to-do list, things that have caused you stress, really aren't all that important.

Who have you been thinking about as you've read this chapter? Perhaps the face of a friend or family member has come to mind, or maybe God has enabled you to see the look in your own eyes. If we try to merely rearrange all the pieces on our life's puzzle, we'll be just as frazzled as before. A better solution is to look to God, to trust him for wisdom and truth, and to reorient our lives according to his love, his purposes, and his Spirit's power in our lives.

━━━━━━━━━━━━━ Healing the Damage ━━━━━━━━━━━━━

1. What are some signs that a woman's constructive, healthy stress has shifted into negative, oppressive stress?

2. What are some signs of impending burnout? What are common causes you've seen in others or in your own life?

3. Read Luke 10:38-42. As we looked at Martha's motives, did your impression of her change? Did the situation and her motives justify her catty attitude? Why or why not?

4. How have advances in technology raised people's expectations for a better life? How have these expectations affected you and your family's attitudes and relationships?

5. Where would you place your life on a scale of -5 (abject burnout) to 0 (a balanced life) to +5 (compulsive busyness)? Explain your answer. Which direction are you moving?

6. How can busyness become a badge of honor? How can helping people with their problems be addictive?

7. Read 1 Peter 5:5-9. What are some reasons humility and faith are essential in overcoming anxiety? How are anxiety and pride related?

8. Write a specific plan to deal with any excessive stress in your life. Address issues of trust in God, carving out time with him, unplugging from technology, saying no to things that aren't priorities, finding fun in life again, exercise, nutrition, and sleep.

====== Bible Passages on Stress and Exhaustion ======

"[Cast] all your anxiety on Him, because He cares for you" (1 Peter 5:7 NASB).

"No temptation has overtaken you but such as is common to man; and God is faithful, who will not allow you to be tempted beyond what you are able, but with the temptation will provide the way of escape also, so that you will be able to endure it" (1 Corinthians 10:13 NASB).

"Anxiety in a man's heart weighs it down,
But a good word makes it glad" (Proverbs 12:25 NASB).

"I will lift up my eyes to the mountains;
From where shall my help come?
My help comes from the LORD,
Who made heaven and earth.
He will not allow your foot to slip;
He who keeps you will not slumber.
Behold, He who keeps Israel
Will neither slumber nor sleep.
The LORD is your keeper;
The LORD is your shade on your right hand.
The sun will not smite you by day,
Nor the moon by night.
The LORD will protect you from all evil;
He will keep your soul.
The LORD will guard your going out and your coming in
From this time forth and forever" (Psalm 121 NASB).

"Be anxious for nothing, but in everything by prayer and supplication with thanksgiving let your requests be made known to God. And the peace of God, which surpasses all comprehension, will guard your hearts and your minds in Christ Jesus" (Philippians 4:6-7 NASB).

"Peace I leave with you; My peace I give to you; not as
the world gives do I give to you. Do not let your heart be
troubled, nor let it be fearful" (John 14:27 NASB).

"God is our refuge and strength,
A very present help in trouble.
Therefore we will not fear, though the earth should change
And though the mountains slip into the heart of the sea;
Though its waters roar and foam,
Though the mountains quake at its swelling pride"
(Psalm 46:1-3 NASB).

"The LORD also will be a stronghold for the oppressed,
A stronghold in times of trouble;
And those who know Your name will put their trust in You,
For You, O LORD, have not forsaken those who seek You"
(Psalm 9:9-10 NASB).

"He gives strength to the weary,
And to him who lacks might He increases power"
(Isaiah 40:29 NASB).

9

$\mathcal{D}$eep $\mathcal{P}$ain

One's real life is often the life that one does not lead.

OSCAR WILDE

I heard about Mary Beth before I actually met her. People called her the sweetest girl in the world. The moment I met her, I had to agree. Mary Beth's sunny disposition almost glowed. As she worked on the leadership team for a women's ministry at a large church, she sincerely and specifically complimented every person's efforts and thanked everyone who did anything for anyone. People loved to be around Mary Beth. But as I watched her, I began to suspect that her constant smile might be hiding something darker in her past.

Over the next couple of weeks, our paths crossed a few times. She had a major responsibility for one of our conferences, and I was in a couple of planning meetings with her. At each one, she lit up the room with her optimism. At one, however, someone brought the bad news that a lady who worked closely with Mary Beth had dropped the ball. She reported, "Sorry, Mary Beth, but now you'll have to do twice the work in half the time."

Mary Beth smiled sweetly and responded, "Oh, I don't mind at all. It's all for the Lord, you know."

Mary Beth was known for her pleasant demeanor, but now it seemed to be a bit too sunny. She refused to acknowledge *any* clouds in her sky. This woman's life seemed to be perfect, but I wondered what was behind her mask of joy. What about the pain? The heartache? The sorrow? What about the ordinary cares and stresses of life? Was she immune?

Don't get me wrong. I love to be around optimistic, hopeful people, but if we are to live in reality, we must acknowledge the difficulties and heartaches we all experience from time to time. A casual reading of the Psalms shows us the writers' full range of emotion, from praise to deep discouragement, from thankfulness to fierce anger. Being optimistic doesn't mean being unrealistic about problems in life. No, it means we trust God even in dark times.

I decided to initiate a conversation with Mary Beth to see where it might go. A few days later, I met her at a coffee shop. We found a secluded booth in the back, and I began by telling her how thankful I was for all of her help on the conference. She smiled and looked down, speaking softly, "It's nothing, really."

I continued, "I'd like to get to know you. Tell me about your family."

She beamed as she told me about her husband and their three children, ages 8 to 17. It seemed to be the perfect family, but I wanted to probe a bit more. "That's wonderful. All of us experience seasons of difficulty. What are some struggles you and your family have gone through?"

She quickly replied, "Oh, none. We're really happy. God has been so good to us."

No problems? That was clearly too good to be true, so I took a different path. "Tell me about your family when you were growing up. What was your dad like, and your mom?"

Her expression instantly changed. She hesitated a bit, and then she told me, "My father tried as hard as he could to be a wonderful father—and he was, he really was. And my mother is a marvelous woman...so dear. I couldn't ask for anything more."

She seemed to hope that was enough information for me, but I continued, "Go on. Tell me more about them. What do you mean that your dad tried to be a wonderful father?"

She paused for a few seconds, and then sheepishly said, "Well, Dad drank a little."

Finally, the tip of the iceberg. "How did his drinking affect him?" I asked. "And how did it affect you?"

Suddenly, Mary Beth's sunny smile completely vanished. In its place was a vacuous, vacant stare. She labored to answer me, but finally she said, "He...he got angry a few times."

"Angry?"

Instantly, she pulled the curtain of her heart closed and defended her father again: "Yes, but he couldn't help it. He didn't mean to hit Mom. It was the alcohol, not him. He really was kind and sweet when he wasn't drinking." After a few more seconds, she blurted out, "Julie, all this is in the past, and I really don't want to talk about it anymore. I've forgiven him, and it doesn't affect me any longer. My life is wonderful today."

I changed the subject to something more pleasant, and we finished our chat. As we parted, Mary Beth was smiling, but I was sure she didn't want to have coffee with me again anytime soon.

Many women have been deeply wounded by abuse or abandonment. Abuse comes in various forms and levels of intensity. It can crush a girl's spirit, or it can be like the needles on a cactus, pricking us over and over again when we come too close. Even though the causes of emotional pain are usually obvious to outside observers, many women don't realize how wounded they are. Their pain is more than they want to face, so they explain it away.

One dictionary defines pain as "physical suffering or distress, as due to injury, illness, etc.; mental or emotional suffering or torment." Sexual abuse includes rape, incest, fondling, or verbal enticements or teasing, and it can happen at any age to anyone. Physical abuse involves hitting, slapping, pushing, pinching, or any other inappropriate and pain-inflicting touch. It also involves any threat of those actions. Verbal abuse covers the gamut of harsh, angry, condemning, blaming messages. All of these—in all their varied forms and range of intensity—inflict emotional wounds on victims. Abandonment is the absence of someone who should be present to give care and protection. This problem occurs when a parent or spouse walks out, but it also leaves a wound when these people are physically present but emotionally absent. Abandonment is, in the opinion of many psychologists, even more difficult to address because there's no face to remember, no person to blame, and seemingly no cause for the gnawing emptiness and confusion we feel.

Those who inflict abuse or abandon us may be parents, other adult relatives, siblings, friends, spouses, children, employers, coworkers, or total strangers. Elder abuse—inflicting harm on the elderly or neglecting to care for them—is increasingly common.

Every woman experiences pain. It's a normal and unavoidable part of living in a sinful, fallen world. Until we get to heaven, where there will be no more crying or hurt or brokenness, life will have its wounds. I've talked to confused women about devastatingly painful events, such as sexual abuse or physical violence, who casually remark, "It only happened a few times. It shouldn't bother me that much."

But how many hits from a man's fist does it take to break a bone? Not many. Really, only one. Sometimes women weep when they realize the pain they feel is completely normal for the abuse they've endured, even if it only happened once or twice. Many women suffer wounds at the hands of others *and* themselves: They are initially and suddenly devastated by sexual or physical abuse, and then a gradual avalanche of negative self-talk drains their confidence and ruins their happiness. Too often, we Christian women feel that we must be strong, confident, and put together, even if our hearts are bleeding from the evil we've suffered at the hands of those we trusted. With the freeing realization that we don't have to hide our pain, we can be free of the lie that we are somehow inferior or inadequate because we hurt. No pain is too big for Jesus to heal, but hiding or ignoring our hurt only slows down the healing process.

Like Mary Beth, many women mask their deep and devastating pain beneath a sunny smile and pervasive optimism. No one knows what they've suffered, and when they close the door in secrecy, they unknowingly close the door to healing. As counselors like to remind us, we are usually as sick as our secrets. When women are asked about what's really going on, the look in their eyes often changes drastically. They want to be free, but they are afraid of condemnation and judgment, so they close the door on their hurts, put on a happy face, and carry their pain to the grave. Alone.

- Every two minutes, someone is sexually assaulted in America.
- Sixty percent of sexual assaults are not reported to the police.[1]
- Fifteen percent of sexual assault and rape victims are under age 12.
- Twenty-nine percent are 12 to 17.
- Eighty percent are under age 30.
- Females aged 12 to 34 are at the highest risk.
- Girls who are 16 to 19 are four times more likely than the general population to be victims of rape, attempted rape, or sexual assault.
- Twenty-nine percent of all women who attempt suicide were battered, 37 percent of battered women have symptoms of depression, 46 percent have symptoms of anxiety disorder, and 45 percent experience post-traumatic stress disorder.[2]

A Tangled Web of Lust and Rape

One of the most important lessons parents can teach their daughters is that not all young men have their best interests at heart. Sometimes, testosterone runs rampant, and young men care only to satisfy their explosive sexual desires. One of the characteristics of the Bible that sets it apart from other ancient writings is that it describes people in graphic and realistic detail. In Egyptian, Hindu, and other texts of ancient times, heroes appear almost like comic-book superhero characters, but the Bible depicts people "warts and all." The historian who wrote 1 and 2 Samuel describes David's painful and destructive family legacy. He committed sexual sin with Bathsheba and covered it up by murdering her husband, Uriah. Though God graciously forgave him, the consequences reverberated into the next generation.

David's eldest son and heir to the throne, Amnon, became fixated on his beautiful half sister Tamar. In fact, he wanted her so badly that he became lovesick thinking about her. He confided his hopes to a friend, Jonadab, and they devised a plot to have Tamar bring dinner to his bedroom. "Go to bed and pretend to be ill," Jonadab said. "When your father comes to see you, say to him, 'I would like my sister Tamar to come and give me something to eat. Let her prepare the food in my sight so I may watch her and then eat it from her hand'" (2 Samuel 13:5).

As a loving sister, Tamar was happy to comply with her father's request. She carefully prepared cakes and took them to Amnon's home, but he refused to eat. He asked everyone else to leave the house, and then he told her, "Bring the food here into my bedroom so I may eat from your hand." She probably didn't suspect a thing, so she dutifully took the food into his bedroom. As she reached out to offer him a cake, Amnon grabbed her and insisted, "Come to bed with me, my sister."

Tamar instantly realized the implications of his demand. "Don't, my brother!" she said to him. "Don't force me. Such a thing should not be done in Israel! Don't do this wicked thing. What about me? Where could I get rid of my disgrace? And what about you? You would be like one of the wicked fools in Israel. Please speak to the king; he will not keep me from being married to you."

But Amnon wasn't interested in her honor; he was consumed with his lust for sex with his beautiful half sister. He refused her request, overpowered her, and raped her.

Lust is a tragic deformity of love. Instead of cherishing the woman he desired, Amnon used her and discarded her. In fact, the act of sexual abuse is the opposite of love. The writer tells us that after he was finished with Tamar, "Amnon hated her with intense hatred. In fact, he hated her more than he had loved her. Amnon said to her, 'Get up and get out!'"

Amazingly, Tamar kept her wits about her. She responded, "No! Sending me away would be a greater wrong than what you have already done to me." But Amnon had no sense of right and wrong. He called his servant to throw her out of the house and bolt the door behind her. Now, fully realizing the devastation, Tamar put ashes of grief on her head and tore the beautiful robe she was wearing. She ran away weeping to her brother Absalom. In a sad and tragic summary, we read, "And Tamar lived in her brother Absalom's house, a desolate woman" (2 Samuel 13:20).

We might have expected more from King David, the man after God's own heart, but when he learned of the rape in his own family, he blew up in anger and then did absolutely nothing. Absalom, however, wasn't content to let his brother off the hook so easily. Later, he carefully devised a plan to murder Amnon, and the cycle of violence continued.

Trust is fragile. When people earn it by consistent honesty and responsible actions, we can relax in the relationship. But when trust is demolished by sledgehammer blows torn by the pricks of a cactus, we rightly withhold our trust and insist that it be earned again. Some of us, though, continue to trust even those whose behavior has demonstrated that they shouldn't be trusted. And conversely, some of us are so wounded that we can't bring ourselves to trust even those who have proven to be honest and reliable again and again.

Instances of abuse or abandonment are seldom isolated instances, especially in families. Quite often, we find a complex web of deceit, lust, rage, selfishness, and previous patterns of sin that form a bleak backdrop to an event, and this complex web prevents healthy resolution. Some of the most courageous women I know are those who have faced these demons—the devastating moments, the tangled web of sin, and the distorted patterns of deception—in their own lives and their families.

Fresh Insights

People who have suffered deep wounds have two goals in life: to protect themselves from additional hurts and to find some sense of meaning. To accomplish these goals, they usually wear masks to hide their pain and play roles to earn approval. These masks and roles can look quite different from person to person because of people's various personalities and circumstances. In his groundbreaking book on sexual abuse *The Wounded Heart*, Christian psychologist Dan Allender describes three ways women try to cope with life after they've been abused. They can apply to any type of abuse or abandonment.

Good girls. Like Mary Beth in the opening story in this chapter, some women conclude that the way to make life work is to always be happy. They assume that if they never say anything critical, no one can be upset with them. They try hard to win acceptance by helping everyone they meet. Sweetness is a defense against potential threats of conflict. These plans, however, prevent them from dealing with the deep hurt in their lives and keep them locked into the pattern of denial, superficial relationship, and blind optimism.

Tough girls. Some women respond in quite the opposite way. With fierce determination, they (actually or metaphorically) look their abusers squarely in the face and assert, "I'll never let that happen again!" The look on their faces is stern. They seem to be in complete control, but they are terribly threatened by people who challenge them. They are determined to win at all costs at work, at home, at church, and everywhere else they go. Their competence and confidence impress most people, and quite often, they get their way. Their anger and defensiveness, however, keep people at arm's length—exactly where tough girls want them.

Party girls. Some women lack the confidence of the tough girl, and they can't bring themselves to be nice all day, every day like the good girl. But they've had more than their share of pain, so they decide to fill their lives with as much fun as possible, regardless of the risks and the cost. These women are the life of the party, willing to try alcohol, drugs, risky sex, and anything else that will bring a thrill for a few minutes. Lots of people want to hang around them, but they have very few if any true friends. Their lives are consumed with the pursuit of passing pleasures. When someone tries to warn them about the painful consequences lurking right around the corner, they just laugh it off. "I'm having a blast!" they insist.

Deeply wounded women like these cling to their masks and roles as long as possible to hide their pain and fill their lives with a semblance of peace and purpose. Gradually, though, these patterns of life take their toll because they can't provide what all of us want most: genuine love and purpose. The roles are only counterfeits of the real thing. I've known good girls who crashed in depression, tough girls who ran off everyone who cared about them and became tragically alone, and party girls who became addicts and lost everything.

The good girl, the tough girl, and the party girl are ultimately all trying to do the same thing: make the pain go away. But ignoring brokenness can't really make us better. Imagine if you shattered a bone but just pretended that everything was fine. The result would be disastrous! More than the initial trauma itself, hidden pain can be extremely destructive.

> The ordinary response to atrocities is to banish them from consciousness...Certain violations of the social compact are too terrible to utter aloud: this is the meaning of the word "unspeakable"...Atrocities, however, refuse to be buried...Remembering and telling the truth about terrible events are prerequisites for the restoration of the social order and for the healing of individual victims...When the truth is finally recognized, survivors can begin their

recovery. But far too often secrecy prevails, and the story of the traumatic event surfaces not as a verbal narrative but as a symptom."[3]

Breaking through the facade and opening the door to God's healing is very difficult, but countless women have done it. They may have entered the healing process for very different reasons—to avoid losing their marriages or their children, to prevent suicide, and to stop hurting other people, for example—but in every case, we find a single common denominator: desperation. They've worked hard to keep their masks in place, but those masks are no longer hiding the truth. They've played their roles as hard and long as they could, but they've come to the ends of their ropes. Now they're facing the cold, hard fact that their lives are in a tailspin, and they cry out for help. That's the essential beginning point, when God can step in and begin to heal the hurts, teach them what love really means, and put the broken pieces of their lives back together (or together for the first time). Is that really possible? Oh yes. I've seen it many, many times in women's lives.

These abused or abandoned women—good girls, tough girls, and party girls—had their own looks in their eyes when they played their roles, but when the healing process begins, the shock of reality stuns them. That's when each one has a vacant stare—for a while. With courage and the support of a friend or two, that vacant look gradually gives way to peace, hope, and love. It's a beautiful thing to see.

Steps Forward

As we experience healing, our view of God changes. Many victims have been hurt by people in authority over them, and they have assumed that God, the highest authority, is just as untrustworthy. God's Word, however, clearly tells us that God is not at all like an abuser and that he cannot possibly abandon his children. One of my favorite passages in the Bible says that God heals the brokenhearted, and the context is particularly significant.

The LORD builds up Jerusalem;
    he gathers the exiles of Israel.
He heals the brokenhearted
    and binds up their wounds.
He determines the number of the stars
    and calls them each by name.
Great is our Lord and mighty in power;
    his understanding has no limit (Psalm 147:2-5).

God can heal our broken hearts because he cares so deeply, he understands every element of our pain and the process of recovery, and he has the power to touch our deepest hurts and bring peace and comfort. And he is a builder. His processes may be slower than we'd like, but we can trust him to take us each step of the way. What God starts, he finishes.

Another beautiful image of God's care for wounded people is in Isaiah's description of the Messiah, who we know is Jesus.

A bruised reed he will not break,
    and a smoldering wick he will not snuff out.
In faithfulness he will bring forth justice;
    he will not falter or be discouraged
till he establishes justice on earth.
    In his law the islands will put their hope
    (Isaiah 42:3-4).

I've talked to many women who blamed God for allowing their abuse to happen or for not making their pain go away. But God isn't to blame. He cries with us in our brokenness. He is angry when his precious daughters suffer evil. He is completely attentive and gentle, unwilling to break a bruised reed or extinguish the tiniest flicker of hope in our hearts. Nothing prevents him from loving us. He wants to bring peace to the earth, a process that takes time and includes bringing comfort to the wounded and justice to those who wounded them.

We can be certain of God's heart and his actions even though his purposes cannot be fulfilled as quickly as we would like. We have to remember that he is the Lord and we are not. And he operates on his timing, not ours. We can trust him to accomplish all he said he would do. Our job is to think rightly about him and let him have his way in us, in our circumstances, and in those who have hurt us.

Some teachers and writers promise quick and complete healing for all our wounds, but clearly, God doesn't usually work that way. Emotional healing is much more like the long, slow process of mending of a broken bone, and some of us have multiple compound fractures! Healing a break includes emergency care, setting the bone in surgery, and months of rehabilitation. In the same way, deeply wounded people need emergency psychological and spiritual care, professional help in separating masks and roles from the truth, and time to grieve and acquire new skills for healthy relationships. We won't make progress, though, if we lie by the side of the road, broken and bleeding. We need to make the call for help and then cooperate with the EMTs to begin the healing process.

As you read this chapter, who came to mind? Did you think of a friend or family member who is still wearing a mask and playing a role instead of experiencing God's healing touch? Or did you see yourself trying to hide your pain behind a smile? Maybe you hurt because of sexual or emotional abuse. Maybe your husband walked out on you. Your situation may be different from these, but it is no less serious. Maybe you've experienced the death of a dear friend, a parent, or even your own child. One of my favorite songs, Natalie Grant's "Held," is about a woman who woke up one morning to find her perfect, eight-month-old baby dead in his nursery. This woman was obviously devastated, but by God's grace, she took her brokenness and pain to God, rather than becoming bitter. "My faith cannot protect me from pain," she said, "but my faith provides me with healing...He didn't promise everything would be easy, but when everything fell, we would be held in his safe and loving arms."[4]

Regardless of the depths of pain you have experienced, God wants to pick up the broken pieces of your heart and heal the hurt.

Healing starts with being honest with your heavenly Father rather than pretending to God and everyone else that you're fine. We hide a lot behind our smiles, but we don't have to. If you have a friend who has been hurt by life, realize that all you can do is offer assistance. You can't make someone act courageously, but perhaps that person trusts you enough to follow your advice.

And if you need help, make the call today. Don't wait any longer to expose the long-hidden wound to someone who can bring God's healing, forgiveness, hope, and love into your life. God is there—right in the middle of your pain. And he might just use a member of his body, the church, to help repair your brokenness. Dare to take off your mask today. Step out of your role. Expose the pain to someone you trust. Sure, it'll hurt, but the healing will be worth it.

Healing the Damage

1. What does "wearing a mask" mean to you? What does the mask say about what may be going on in the person's mind and heart?

2. What are some ways women try to minimize the damage caused by abuse or abandonment? What excuses do women give for the people who hurt them?

3. Read the story of Amnon and Tamar in 2 Samuel 13. Did Tamar deserve what happened to her? Why or why not? Does any abuse victim deserve what happened to her? Explain your answer.

4. Describe the behavior, motivations, and the look in the eyes of the good girl, the tough girl, and the party girl.

5. Read Psalm 147:2-5. Why is it important to reflect on

the character of God as we consider his desire to heal the brokenhearted?

6. Read Isaiah 42:3-4. Who do you know who needs God's healing touch? What do their eyes look like today?

7. Compare and contrast healing from abuse and healing from a compound fracture.

Bible Passages on Deep Pain

"He heals the brokenhearted
    and binds up their wounds" (Psalm 147:3).

"Those who wait for the LORD
Will gain new strength;
They will mount up with wings like eagles,
They will run and not get tired,
They will walk and not become weary"
(Isaiah 40:31 NASB).

"Do not fear, for I am with you;
Do not anxiously look about you, for I am your God.
I will strengthen you, surely I will help you,
Surely I will uphold you with My righteous right hand"
(Isaiah 41:10 NASB).

"When you pass through the waters, I will be with you;
And through the rivers, they will not overflow you.
When you walk through the fire, you will not be scorched,
Nor will the flame burn you" (Isaiah 43:2 NASB).

"So the ransomed of the LORD will return
And come with joyful shouting to Zion,
And everlasting joy will be on their heads.

They will obtain gladness and joy,
And sorrow and sighing will flee away"
(Isaiah 51:11 NASB).

"Blessed be the God and Father of our Lord Jesus Christ,
the Father of mercies and God of all comfort, who com-
forts us in all our affliction so that we will be able to comfort those who are in any affliction with the comfort with
which we ourselves are comforted by God" (2 Corinthians
1:3-4 NASB).

"For this reason I also suffer these things, but I am not
ashamed; for I know whom I have believed and I am convinced that He is able to guard what I have entrusted to
Him until that day" (2 Timothy 1:12 NASB).

10

Blind Spots: Eyes Wide Shut

The surest way to be deceived is to
consider oneself cleverer than others.

FRANCOIS DE LA ROCHEFOUCAULD

As we get older (or should I say, more mature), our vision gradually but inevitably suffers: night blindness, cataracts, macular degeneration…Our eyes get tired, and we're forced to embrace the fashion of bifocals. (But sometimes I still find myself squinting to read a menu or a price tag.)

My blind spots remind me of one of the sweetest, strongest spiritual mentors God blessed me with—Tim's mom. One day as Tim was filling our car with gas, the station attendant hesitantly asked him, "So what's going on with your mom, Tim? Is she all right?"

A bit confused, Tim responded, "What do you mean?"

"Well, people are worried about her. She drives 20 miles an hour, and she swerves a lot. It's getting dangerous." Perplexed and worried, Tim questioned his mom and found out her vision was getting worse. Diabetes was stealing her sight.

As time went on, my mother-in-law's eyes continued to degenerate. Driving was soon out of the picture. I remember when we took our newborn son, Zach, to Tim's parents for the first time. She cocked her head and squinted her eyes, tracing the outlines of his little nose and forehead with her weathered hands. "It's like looking through muddy water," she told us. "But he looks like my Tim. I know it. He looks like my Tim." In spite of a horrible journey of degenerating vision, she had an amazing ability to see and feel her way.

But have you ever met people who were just the opposite? People who would listen to what you had to say but just not get it?

Totally Clueless

In my conversations with women all over the country, I've seen the old adage proven true over and over: People have an almost limitless capacity for self-deception. Some of us can see just fine, but *we lie to ourselves*. A lot. Does that sound harsh? It's true. Many times, in the midst of pain, trying to make sense of life is not all that different from looking through eyes full of muddy water.

Not long ago, I met with Suzanne. She was a young mother of three, and she looked tired and distressed. When she called to invite me to lunch, she intimated that she wanted to talk to me about something that was going wrong in her marriage. After a few pleasantries, I said, "Suzanne, tell me what's going on."

Her eyes filled with tears as she painstakingly related the history of her relationship with Phillip. She told me that he had been abusing prescription drugs and alcohol since the beginning of their marriage. Now, with three young children and an out-of-control husband, the stress of life threatened to overwhelm Suzanne. She told me story after story of Phillip wrecking the car, passing out while he was watching the children, falling down the stairs, skipping payments on bills, and lying.

I asked, "How have you tried to handle the problem? Have you talked to him about the damage it's doing to you and the kids?"

Again, tears filled her eyes, and she replied, "Oh, not until lately. He just needs to know he's loved. If he was convinced of that, I'm sure he'd change. He has had such a horrible life. I've just tried to be loving and supportive through all of this." She had lived with an alcoholic and drug addict for 15 years without boldly addressing the issue!

Then she told me, "My father was an alcoholic, and I swore I'd never marry anyone who drank or used drugs." She paused, wiped a tear, and then continued, "Julie, I don't know what to do. I'm going crazy. I hate my life. Help!"

I tried to retain a measured voice, but I'm not sure I did very well as I offered her my best advice. "Suzanne, I've seen a lot of women in situations like yours who found hope and help. They had been in bondage in a relationship with an addict, but now they're enjoying life more than they ever imagined."

"That's encouraging," she smiled, "but I'd prefer not using the word 'addict' to talk about Phillip."

Instead of responding to that, I continued. "But these brave women decided they'd base their lives on truth—not what they wanted to believe or wished was true, but on the facts of their lives. Without a commitment to truth, they had no chance of moving forward." That comment seemed to surprise her, but I continued, "Suzanne, your husband's greatest need isn't tenderness and love. He needs to be a man, to take responsibility for his actions, and to protect and provide for you and the children. Nothing else and nothing less." She seemed shocked that I hadn't bought her line about him just needing to know he is loved. I had said some hard things to her, but I wasn't through. I explained, "And you need to start taking care of yourself, setting boundaries, feeding your mind and heart with truth, and experiencing God's healing—regardless of whether Phillip ever changes."

For their entire marriage, Suzanne had been tiptoeing around Phillip's addiction (and yes, he was addicted). She had been deceived about who he was before they married, and she was deceived about how to handle the situation as a Christian wife. She thought being submissive meant never saying anything that might upset him. Our first conversation wasn't the time and place to explain all the details of their potential recovery. She probably absorbed only a fraction of what I said to her, but that's okay. She was just beginning her discovery of truth. I suggested that she see a professional counselor and begin attending a support group. "If you'll do those things," I assured her, "the lights will gradually come on for you."

You may read Suzanne's story and think, *How could she be so blind? Girl, you need to knock that boy out!* Or you may think, *Julie, you were so harsh with her! Can't you see that she's just trying to love Phillip?* To some degree, all of us have blind spots. It's part of being human. But we should pursue wisdom, insight, and understanding with all our might. They will lead to growth in every aspect of our development.

Giving up our false reality and choosing to see things the way they really are can be messy, inconvenient, and threatening. Most of us have gotten used to the way things are and figured out how to make them work for us to some degree. If we live in chaos, chaos becomes familiar and predictable. Occasionally, we get a hint that we might not have the full picture, but change can be unsettling, so we choose to run back to the safety of the familiar as soon as possible. Instead recognizing that we are responsible for our own lives, we conveniently blame others for our problems.

In Solomon's prologue in Proverbs, he writes, "The fear of the LORD is the beginning of knowledge, but fools despise wisdom and discipline" (Proverbs 1:7). *Despise?* We can take this important word in a couple of ways. We usually think that to despise someone or something includes a measure of anger, but it may only imply preferring one thing over another. Fools, then, may angrily reject and detest God's wisdom, or they may simply look at the choices and pick ridiculous options instead of following God's path for them. Why in the world would we do that? Because the deceptions are so attractive! We want to believe the lies because they promise to make us happy, successful, and popular.

We may be naive about friends or employers, thinking they genuinely care about us when they're actually saying nice things to manipulate us for selfish gain. Or on the other hand, we may foolishly withdraw from honest, loving people because we refuse to take even the smallest risk in relationships.

We may be foolish in our relationships with men, trusting them because we desperately want them to be trustworthy even though they've shown that they just aren't that into us.

We may be less than objective about ourselves, thinking we're indestructible when we're young and indispensable when we're older. Or we may become so depressed that we forget that God loves us dearly and has equipped us to make a difference in the world.

We may have blind spots about God, thinking that he's like the parent who hurt us terribly when we were young, or that he should be a Santa Claus and fulfill our every whim.

In our culture, we have to fight like mad to keep from being deceived about what's really important in life. Everything around us screams that beauty, wealth, and prestige are what's really important, but Jesus had a very different message. Think about the most popular television programs and movies. In many cases, writers and actors make the sins of adultery, murder, and raw ambition look thoroughly desirable. Many of us watch and don't have a second thought. We subconsciously soak up the message without even contemplating the value, relevance, or ethics of the stories. Solomon's words about his own culture could easily apply to our own: "A fool finds pleasure in evil conduct, but a man of understanding delights in wisdom" (Proverbs 10:23).

We continue operating according to our perceptions for the simple reason that they make perfect sense to us. We naturally see things and embrace assumptions and interpretations that reinforce our particular vision of life. So over time, our blind spots may even become bigger, not smaller—until something happens that rocks our world and causes us to sit up and look at life from a different point of view. Sometimes, the truth is unsettling because it chips away at our self-created, unrealistic view of the world. What we feel seems to be so right, and everyone else's interpretations seem so very wrong. But remember, girls, we're all human, and we're all prone to developing blind spots.

> What you see and hear depends a good deal on where you are standing; it also depends on what sort of person you are.
>
> C.S. LEWIS

Our Sister Eve

The first sin could have happened to anyone, and in fact, it represents what happens to everyone! It is much like every sin that has happened since: A willing ear listened to a deceptive voice and took action that led to tragedy.

Talk about a sweet life—Adam and Eve had it all. They had great weather, great food, and total freedom. No worries. Who could ask for more than that? No guilt, no second-guessing their choices. They enjoyed living in the presence of God and fulfilling his plan. God gave them everything they could possibly need in order to live with joy, adventure, and contentment...including a single restriction: "And the LORD God commanded the man, 'You are free to eat from any tree in the garden; but you must not eat from the tree of the knowledge of good and evil, for when you eat of it you will surely die'" (Genesis 2:16-17).

But another voice spoke into Eve's ear. The serpent questioned God's directive by asking her, "Did God really say, 'You must not eat from any tree in the garden'?" (Genesis 3:1). To her credit, Eve corrected the serpent, but she added a bit more to the command than God had spoken. She told the serpent that God restricted them from touching the tree. He didn't say that. I don't know if her misstatement was the thin edge of the wedge that separated her from wisdom at that moment, but immediately, the serpent jumped in. "'You will not surely die,' the serpent said to the woman. 'For God knows that when you eat of it your eyes will be opened, and you will be like God, knowing good and evil'" (verses 4-5).

The rest, as they say, is history. Eve trusted the liar, looked at the fruit on the tree, and believed that eating it would make her as wise as God. But the real lure for Eve was the promise that she could be like God. What does that mean? Perhaps her temptation was just like the ones we face every day: to run our own lives, to be supreme in our worlds, and to be free from any constraints or demands. Sounds good, doesn't it? It certainly sounded good to Eve, so she gave in and ate the fruit, and we've suffered the devastating results since that day. Tim often jokingly reminds me, "Eve ate first." But let's face it: Adam knew exactly what he was doing when he sinned. (I just wanted to point that out.)

If our sister Eve could experience a huge blind spot and believe a lie in a perfect environment with all her needs met, what chance do we have of walking perfectly in truth? Satan undoubtedly whispers in our ears just as loudly and clearly as he spoke to Eve, but today, he uses the voices of friends, coworkers, family members, the media, and our own distorted desires to promise delights he can't deliver.

We can reduce our blind spots by giving attention to the truth of God's Word, following the prompting of his Spirit, and spending time with mature believers who model a life of truth and faith for us. I wish we could instantly download and install perception software, but life doesn't work that way. Gaining God's insights is a long, sometimes difficult journey, but we can make remarkable progress if we stay on the path and remain immersed in the Scriptures, empowered by the Spirit, and connected with fellow pilgrims.

> The voyage of discovery is not in seeking new
> landscapes but in having new eyes.
> MARCEL PROUST

Fresh Insights

How important is objective truth in our lives? More than 75 times in the Gospels, the writers quote Jesus saying, "I tell you the truth." When Jesus stood before Pilate on the day he was killed, he told the governor that he came to "testify to the truth." Whenever Jesus spoke, whether to prostitutes or governors, rich or poor, the powerful or the weak, he always spoke the truth. Sometimes he spoke of God's incredible kindness and grace, but sometimes the truth cut like a knife. He called the unbelieving religious leaders of his day a brood of vipers and whitewashed tombs that looked good on the outside but were rotten inside. He didn't mince words with anyone but was completely appropriate to each situation. To the woman caught in adultery, he said, "Neither do I condemn you. Go and sin no more," but to the Pharisees who resisted his message of grace, he proclaimed,

> If God were your Father, you would love me, for I came from God and now am here. I have not come on my own; but he sent me. Why is my language not clear to you? Because you are unable to hear what I say. You belong to your father, the devil, and you want to carry out your father's desire. He was a murderer from the beginning, not holding to the truth, for there is no truth in him. When he lies, he speaks his native language, for he is a liar and the father of lies. Yet because I tell the truth, you do not believe me! Can any of you prove me guilty of sin? If I am telling the truth, why don't you believe me? He who belongs to God hears what God says. The reason you do not hear is that you do not belong to God (John 8:42-47).

If our version of truth doesn't include both grace and justice, it's off base, watered down, and ineffective in addressing the full range of problems and opportunities we face. In the story at the beginning of this chapter, Suzanne's brand of truth was full of warmth for her husband but didn't include a request for him to be responsible for his behavior.

One of the marks of a mature faith is the ability to recognize satanic lies and cultural deceptions. The process of spiritual growth inevitably involves identifying and rejecting falsehood and replacing it with truth. In Paul's letters, he took pains to point out wrong thinking, false hopes, and lies of every kind. Consider this passage to the believers in Colossae:

> So then, just as you received Christ Jesus as Lord, continue to live in him, rooted and built up in him, strengthened in the faith as you were taught, and overflowing with thankfulness. See to it that no one takes you captive through hollow and deceptive philosophy, which depends on human tradition and the basic principles of this world rather than on Christ (Colossians 2:6-8).

Captive? Is that an accurate image of those who believe deceptions? Yes, I think it is. When we try to get ahead at all costs, put down others to elevate ourselves, and escape hard realities instead of trusting God to guide us through them, everything in us gets wrapped up in lies. These false notions consume our thoughts, dominate our feelings, and dictate our behavior.

We long for an easy life. Maybe we've hit a long, hard stretch, and we just want relief. Perhaps we grew up in the center of our parents' world, and we expect to stay in the center of someone's world the rest of our lives. Or we may have listened to teachers who told us that God wants all of us to enjoy an effortless, prosperous life. To be sure, God often gives us relief from suffering, love among family and friends, and a measure of prosperity, but these are gifts, not rights we can demand.

When Jesus was asked what is the greatest commandment in all of Scripture, he responded that it was simply to love the Lord with all our heart, soul, and mind, and to love our neighbors as ourselves. As believers, our consuming purpose in life is first to know, love, and honor God, and then to love others. All the blessings God gives are secondary and transitory. Sometimes we enjoy them, and sometimes we don't, but God's grace, peace, presence, and power can be ours all day, every day.

I'm certainly not saying that heartaches don't matter and hard times don't count. They do. But God wants to use even those to get our attention and teach us more about him, about us, and about his purpose for our lives. When we understand this simple truth, many of our blind spots diminish, and we learn what it means to lose our lives for his sake.

> Truth is universal. Perception of truth is not.
>
> ANONYMOUS

Steps Forward

All of us have blind spots, but we don't have to let them ruin our perception any longer. We gain insight three different ways: We read the Bible and gain insights from God's Word, we watch people and see the benefits of good choices and the consequences of bad ones, and we learn from our own mistakes and face the consequences of our blindness. I'd rather learn from other people's mistakes than make my own, and even better, I'd prefer to learn from God himself.

Eve's blind spot caused her to doubt God's perfect design for her life. She thought she could run her life better than God could. I'm afraid I have the same thought from time to time, and it always gets me into trouble. As God gradually opens our eyes, we see him as he really is, in all of his tenderness and awesome majesty, and we learn to trust him more. When we are tempted to doubt his plan, we remember his character, and we trust him to guide us in his paths and in his timing. When guilt or bitterness clouds our hearts because of the way we have treated others or they have treated us, we remember that Christ's death on the cross pays for all sins— theirs and ours. When we're confused about somebody or a choice we face, we remember that God is the source of understanding and that we can trust him.

Perception makes a world of difference. We desperately need to see God's purpose in every circumstance in our lives. In his book

Reaching for the Invisible God, Philip Yancey recounts, "Gregory of Nyssa once called St. Basil's faith 'ambidextrous' because he welcomed pleasures with the right hand and afflictions with the left, convinced both would serve God's design for him."[1] When we have more insight about the character of God, we gain "ambidextrous faith," trusting God in the good times and the bad to teach us valuable lessons and shape us into the image of Christ.

My dad's passing at 61 rocked my world. I was a daddy's girl. And none of this made any sense. My kids wouldn't even get to know the man I affectionately called Dad. Though I knew without a shadow of doubt that he was rejoicing in heaven, his death shook me to the core. Some days, I missed him so bad I didn't even want to get out of bed, but looking back now, I can see how God used this loss to make my faith more ambidextrous.

Blind spots happen. Discouragement will come. The important thing is to keep focusing our eyes on Jesus. He knows our weakness, and he also knows exactly what our weary souls need before we even ask him! Blind spots can cause us to be naive or foolish in our relationships, careers, habits, and the like, but ultimately, the most important perception is that Jesus deserves every ounce of our devotion.

Paul used Eve's life as a warning that we can be led astray: "I am afraid that just as Eve was deceived by the serpent's cunning, your minds may somehow be led astray from your sincere and pure devotion to Christ" (2 Corinthians 11:3). Countless messages we hear each day threaten to lead us astray, to deceive us and distract us from focusing on Christ. Our goal isn't happiness, wealth, health, or popularity. God may give us those gifts to enjoy, but knowing, loving, obeying, and honoring Jesus Christ is our highest and purest purpose. That's the insight God wants all of us to have. In the next chapter, we'll explore more deeply the meaning of living with clear eyes of faith.

Has the face of a friend or family member come to mind as

you've read this chapter? Or have you been gazing in the mirror? Don't be alarmed to think that you have blind spots. We all do. Thank the Lord for letting you see reality! Let God's Spirit, his Word, and maybe an honest friend speak truth into your life, and then respond in the way God leads you. When you can see clearly, the whole world opens up to you.

Healing the Damage

1. How would you define or describe blind spots in people's lives? How do they get there? Why do we continue to have them even though we read the Bible, pray for wisdom, and dialogue with other believers?

2. What are some differences between people who are naive and those who are foolish? How might each one respond to truth?

3. Read Genesis 2:15–3:7. Jot down the sequence of events that led to Eve's sinful choice. What does being like God mean to us today?

4. Read Colossians 2:6-8. What are some specific ways deception captivates people?

5. What does the phrase *ambidextrous faith* mean to you?

6. As you read this chapter, did you have any fresh insights about your important relationships, your view of God, your sense of purpose, or anything else that might help you overcome a blind spot? If so, what next step can you take to benefit from these insights?

Bible Passages on Blind Spots

"You did not receive the spirit of slavery to fall back into fear, but you have received the Spirit of adoption as sons, by whom we cry, 'Abba! Father!'" (Romans 8:15 ESV).

"O send out Your light and Your truth, let them lead me;
Let them bring me to Your holy hill
And to Your dwelling places" (Psalm 43:3 NASB).

"Behold, You desire truth in the innermost being,
And in the hidden part You will make me know wisdom"
(Psalm 51:6 NASB).

"He who practices the truth comes to the Light, so that his deeds may be manifested as having been wrought in God" (John 3:21 NASB).

"For the wrath of God is revealed from heaven against all ungodliness and unrighteousness of men who suppress the truth in unrighteousness...They exchanged the truth of God for a lie, and worshiped and served the creature rather than the Creator, who is blessed forever. Amen" (Romans 1:18,25 NASB).

"If we go on sinning willfully after receiving the knowledge of the truth, there no longer remains a sacrifice for sins" (Hebrews 10:26 NASB).

11

*P*ursuing *P*erception: A *C*lear-Eyed *F*aith

Blessed are they who see beautiful things in
humble places where other people see nothing.

CAMILLE PISSARRO

*Y*ou have probably never heard of my hometown—Sidney, Montana. You may never have been to Montana at all. The state's population is about 967,000. Some say Montana has more cattle than people. But Montana is known as the Big Sky State. On a clear night, the sky is majestic. Truly, the heavens declare the glory of God.

Over the course of my life, I've had the privilege of seeing the glory of God in the lives of women who faced damaged emotions in their past, daunting obstacles in the present, and promising opportunities in the future with clear-eyed faith in God. This has been a privilege for me because I have learned so much from these women about walking in faith. I've been with them when they heard news all of us dread: "The lump in your breast is cancer." "Your son was in a terrible car accident." "I'm afraid the baby's heart isn't beating any longer." Certainly, the news was devastating, but these faith-filled women faced these realities and wept in grief without self-pity or bitterness. Through the darkest moments in their lives, they held tightly to God, trusting his goodness, direction, and strength.

Were these women deeply hurt? Of course. But in their suffering, *they didn't give up hope*. In the midst of their brokenness and tears, they looked to God rather than trying to make sense of the pain themselves. The look in these women's eyes revealed their inner calm and confidence—not that everything would turn out the way they wanted, but that they could trust God regardless. Even when life hurts (and maybe especially when life hurts!), women who trust God know that he is walking with them, sharing in their tears and fears, and working for their good. Even if the refining process hurts like crazy, Scripture promises that the end will be good—that God will test and refine our faith and bring us closer to Jesus. God always finishes what he starts working on, so you can be confident he will complete his good work in you (Philippians 1:6). And he loves bringing beauty out of ashes!

I have also seen God's daughters whose faith has propelled them to attempt great things for God. They so believed in God's amazing grace that they truly wanted to honor him in everything they did. When they looked around, they saw other women lost and struggling, like sheep without a shepherd, and they sensed God calling them to help in any way they could.

Now, to be honest, I've also seen a look in some leaders' eyes that has scared me. Their expression revealed their desire for personal fame instead of humble service. Those with genuine, Christ-centered faith were amazingly bold, but they took action out of a heart of compassion, not arrogance.

When I think about women of God who not only look to Jesus in the midst of pain but also look for ways to help others, one word comes to my mind: *wisdom*. Their perception of God, of themselves, of tragedy, and of open doors is based on an accurate and hopeful view of reality. Webster's defines wisdom as "knowledge, and the capacity to make due use of it; knowledge of the best ends and the best means; discernment and judgment; discretion; sagacity; skill; dexterity." We can shorten this definition to say it's applied knowledge, insight in action, or perhaps the courage to face reality and respond in faith.

Wisdom doesn't come easily. It's not standard equipment when we come from the womb! As we saw in the last chapter, Solomon reminds us that the source of true wisdom is a deep reverence for God. And Paul explains that wisdom is at the heart of all of his communications with new believers: "My purpose is that they may be encouraged in heart and united in love, so that they may have the full riches of complete understanding, in order that they may know the mystery of God, namely, Christ, in whom are hidden all the treasures of wisdom and knowledge" (Colossians 2:2-3). "The full riches of complete understanding"—that's what Paul wanted people to get from his ministry. And what is the ultimate source? All the treasures of wisdom and knowledge are hidden in Christ.

Hidden treasures fascinate us. They promise untold riches, but finding them takes time, energy, and determination. The women I know who have true perception about God and life understand this search very well. Without exception, they are women who are deeply committed to study God's Word. They don't just read a verse or two, close the book, and go on with their day. Instead, they search for God's meaning in a passage, digging deeper to explore how the truth applies to them and then boldly taking action according to God's wisdom.

The light of God's truth shines on the deepest motives of their hearts and the most entrenched behaviors. Instead of escaping pain by watching too much television, eating, or shopping, wise women face their pain and experience God's gradual healing of their deepest hurts. Instead of being driven to prove their worth by accomplishing more than anyone else, they thank God for their strengths and affirm others who are trying to do the right things for the right reasons. Instead of compulsively controlling people because their own lives are out of control, they learn to trust God and let people make their own choices. Instead of pursuing an elusive peace through affluence, prestige, and possessions, they experience genuine contentment in God's love and purpose, whether they have plenty or little.

When others ridicule these wise women, ignore them, or gossip about them, they don't take revenge by responding in kind. Instead, they choose to offer the divine branch of forgiveness. They face calamity with a tenacious trust in God's goodness, and they explore opportunities out of a heart of gratitude for all God has done for them and a sincere compassion for others. All of these transitions come from God's Word sinking deep into our hearts and transforming our lives from the inside out.

Amazing Abigail

One member of the great cloud of witnesses I can't wait to meet when I go to heaven is Abigail. She was a remarkable woman. The history of Israel tells us she stepped between two hotheaded men, spoke truth with grace, and stopped a murderous rage. She is the epitome of clear-eyed faith.

Abigail's husband, Nabal, was a wealthy rancher near the hilly coastal city of Carmel. When King Saul was chasing David and his men around the country trying to kill them, David looked for friends anywhere he could find them. For a while, some of his men lived near Nabal's flocks, protecting the sheep from wolves and thieves. When it was time for Nabal to shear his sheep, David sent ten men to ask Nabal for help. After all, they had served faithfully without asking for anything in return. But now, David and his men needed a friend who could provide some needed sustenance for them. Though Nabal was fabulously rich and could have easily spared plenty of food for David and his men, he turned them down with studied insults.

David was a great leader, but at this point in his life, he was under intense pressure. One wrong move meant death for him and his followers. His men had served Nabal, but now the rich man wouldn't lift a finger to help them. When David heard the news, he blew up! He told his men to put on their swords, and he led 400 of them toward Carmel to make Nabal pay for his insolence.

Someone told Abigail that David was coming. She could have hidden in fear, or she could have sided with one or the other. In fact, when I think about her life with such a cruel husband, I'm surprised she didn't see this moment as a golden opportunity to get rid of Nabal. If David killed him, she would be completely guiltless, and she'd never have to suffer his abuse again. But Abigail didn't hide or join David's attack. She responded with true wisdom.

She knew that David and his men desperately needed provisions, so she quickly loaded donkeys with bread, wine, sheep, grain, raisins, and cakes of figs—a feast for David and his men. She rode ahead to meet David before he reached Nabal, and there, she diffused his rage with her generous gift and kind words. She didn't argue with David, and she didn't defend her husband's cruelty, but she begged David to accept her gift of food for him and his men. With remarkable diplomacy, she reminded David of his future role as king of Israel. Her words recalled memories of David's victory over Goliath, and she acknowledged his plight as he fled from Saul. But she encouraged him to stop because he needed a clear conscience when he became king.

> Even though someone is pursuing you to take your life, the life of my master will be bound securely in the bundle of the living by the Lord your God. But the lives of your enemies he will hurl away as from the pocket of a sling. When the Lord has done for my master every good thing he promised concerning him and has appointed him leader over Israel, my master will not have on his conscience the staggering burden of needless bloodshed or of having avenged himself. And when the Lord has brought my master success, remember your servant (1 Samuel 25:29-31).

I can almost see David's face transform as he listened to Abigail.

His fierce rage gradually melted into relaxed calm as he understood her reasoning and saw her kindness and strength.

> Praise be to the Lord, the God of Israel, who has sent you today to meet me. May you be blessed for your good judgment and for keeping me from bloodshed this day and from avenging myself with my own hands. Otherwise, as surely as the Lord, the God of Israel, lives, who has kept me from harming you, if you had not come quickly to meet me, not one male belonging to Nabal would have been left alive by daybreak (verses 32-34).

David accepted Abigail's gift of food, thanked her, and sent her back home.

This moment, however, isn't the end of the story. God honored Abigail's faith in a dramatic way (one that I certainly can't guarantee for other abused women who act wisely). The next day wasn't a good one for Nabal: He woke up with a hangover, he heard about Abigail's encounter with David, and he suffered a massive heart attack. A few days later, he died. When David heard the news, he asked Abigail to marry him.

I marvel at Abigail's wisdom. When I feel caught between two powerful people, I usually want to run and hide or control the situation so the conflict goes away. Abigail didn't do either of those. She realized the situation was dangerous, took quick action to meet David's need, and appealed to reason based on his future. She didn't demand that he comply with her wishes, and she didn't hide in fear and hope the problem would go away. Her insight about the situation was mixed with healthy doses of humility and boldness, and God honored her.

> In all perception of the truth there is a divine
> ecstasy, an inexpressible delirium of joy.
> HENRY DAVID THOREAU

Wisdom is an incredibly attractive and powerful trait in a woman's life, but too often, we simply react to people and situations instead of seeing them through the lenses of faith. We may hear sermons every week, attend Bible studies, and read the Bible regularly, but some of us don't let God's truth penetrate our hearts and give us eyes of faith. Our responses to wounds, difficulties, and opportunities sometimes reveal the painful truth that we don't really believe that God loves us, that he has the power or will to change our lives, and that his way is best. Our posteriors may be planted on church pews or Bible-study chairs, but the eyes of our hearts are still clouded by petty selfishness and fear. The writer to the Hebrews tells us, "Without faith it is impossible to please God, because anyone who comes to him must believe that he exists and that he rewards those who earnestly seek him" (Hebrews 11:6). I have to look in the mirror as I say these words: Sometimes we live as if God doesn't even exist. Our feelings tell us we're totally alone, hopeless, and helpless, and we believe our emotions instead of God's Word. Here are three important truths that will help us live with perceptive faith.

I belong to God.

God isn't distant or apathetic, heartless or cruel. The poet Francis Thompson portrayed God as "the hound of heaven" who pursues us. After he catches us, he adopts us into his family, making us coheirs with Christ and showering his love on us. The prophet Isaiah tells us we are inscribed on the palms of God's hands—a figurative way of saying God could never forget us. God is all-knowing and all-seeing. We live under his loving gaze 24 hours a day, seven days a week. When we are at our best, he celebrates with us. When we're at our worst, he invites us to trust him for direction and strength. Paul wrote to the Corinthian believers that we've been bought with a price, so we're no longer our own. We don't have to wander around trying to find a place in life. We have an incredible place as daughters of the King—loved, forgiven, accepted, and equipped to have an impact for him in the lives of people around us.

We can easily sense God is with us when we're singing praise songs on Sunday morning, but he's no less present when we're doing our hair, changing diapers, or writing contracts. When we feel confused, we can trust him to give us direction. When we feel angry, we can ask him to help us deal with the source of our anger. When we feel hopeless, we can thank him for always caring for us and working to accomplish his good purposes in us.

We are naturally self-absorbed. We want what we want when we want it, but this demanding attitude actually keeps us from receiving our hearts' desires. We want to feel special and appreciated, but we push people away and make them afraid of us. However, when we realize we belong to God, we can relax, release our demands, and trust him to bring good out of every situation in our lives. We certainly can't guarantee that everything will turn out just as we wanted, but we can be sure that God will weave a lovely fabric out of the broken threads of our lives.

Every difficult moment and every opportunity is a test that God has designed to strengthen me.

James and Peter both warned us not to be surprised when we encounter trials. Difficulties are a way of life until we see Jesus face-to-face. Our trials come in all shapes and sizes, all degrees, and at any time. Sometimes they suddenly overcome us as tragedies, and sometimes they stand before us as open doors that dare us to walk through them. Regardless of the particulars, they are all tests that God uses to shape our lives.

Most of us don't like tests, but we didn't get through school by avoiding them. We had to face them or flunk. God is our great Teacher. He tests us for good purposes, not to tear us down, and he never gives us tests that are too hard for us to handle. They sometimes seem overwhelming, but he offers us the courage to face them.

Spiritual tests are like the tests we took in school. They show us where we're doing well and where we need improvement. Early in our Christian lives, the tests deal with obvious behaviors like telling the truth or lying, encouraging others or condemning them. But in the higher grades of Christian experience, God tests our motives to see whom we really want to receive the attention—him or us. Every test is an opportune teachable moment, not a meaningless and hopeless calamity. And every test comes from our good, loving, and wise God. He uses these situations to accomplish his purposes in our lives and offers his assistance at every step along the way.

If we think difficulties are aberrations in our lives, we'll resist them and resent God for letting them happen to us. A heart of faith eventually accepts each one as a stepping-stone toward maturity.

I will follow God's leading.

We may want to escape difficult situations and bask in comfort all day every day, but that's a fairyland, not real life. The Christian pilgrimage is the most thrilling adventure life can offer, but adventures mix danger and tedium. God is a loving Father who knows what's best for us, and if we pay attention, he guides us by his Spirit, through his Word, and with the advice of mature friends. Sometimes, like Abigail, we need to take immediate action, but often, God instructs us to wait. During this time, he prepares us for the difficulties ahead, and he prepares others that we will interact with. When we want to withdraw from someone who hurt us, God may direct us to step back into the relationship and share the truth with that person. When we want revenge, God instructs us to forgive. When people around us are in need, God fills us with his love for them and energizes us with his Spirit so we can minister in his name. Sometimes he tells us to rest for a while, and sometimes he changes our course so we can serve more effectively.

God doesn't necessarily give us clear directions the moment we ask for them. We often must pursue him and his leading. His lack of response isn't disinterest; it's his way of maintaining our hunger for him and his purposes. Clear-eyed faith doesn't require God to jump through our hoops. It trusts that God will lead us, and that trust grows as God leads in different ways.

> Your opinion is your opinion, your perception is your perception. Do not confuse them with facts or truth.
>
> JOHN MOORE

Steps Forward

We live in a world of distractions and deceptions. It's the water we swim in, and we're foolish if we think we can swim here without getting wet! Some women learned wisdom from their parents, and they're passing on practical knowledge to their children and friends. Other women grew wise the hard way, starting from square one and building the foundation of their lives on God's truth. Slowly, painfully, they turned from foolish attitudes and actions to become wise. They are heroes to me.

Change doesn't come by magic or from a holy zap. True change comes little by little as God's truth transforms our concepts of him, of ourselves, and of life. After describing God's infinite grace in the first 11 chapters of his letter to the believers in Rome, Paul wrote this:

> Therefore, I urge you, brothers, in view of God's mercy, to offer your bodies as living sacrifices, holy and pleasing to God—this is your spiritual act of worship. Do not conform any longer to the pattern of this world, but be transformed by the renewing of your mind. Then you will be able to test and approve what God's will is—his good, pleasing and perfect will (Romans 12:1-2).

The Greek word translated *transformed* is the same word we use to describe the process of metamorphosis, in which a larva in a chrysalis becomes a beautiful butterfly. How does this dramatic process work in us? By the renewing of our minds as God's truth sinks deep into the crevasses of our thoughts, desires, motives, attitudes, and actions.

Most of us often make resolutions of various kinds, particularly at New Year's but also on other occasions. These resolutions become reality only if we are committed to a process of change. Halfhearted efforts won't do. We need tenacity, clear goals, and confidence that our efforts will yield wonderful benefits. We often think of this kind of commitment when we want to drop a dress size or two, but we also need it in order to allow God to renew our minds. The benefits of wisdom are enormous. We worry less, handle money more wisely, enjoy friends more fully, and find far more contentment and excitement than ever before—but these things don't happen through osmosis as we sit in church. They come only by engaging our minds and hearts with God's will and his ways.

When we open the Bible, some of us feel as if we've picked up a Russian newspaper. We're sure it makes sense to somebody, but it doesn't make much sense to us. So we put it down and carry on without learning a thing. But a little effort in reading the Scriptures produces incredible results. To grasp the truth of the Bible, you have to understand who the author of each book was writing to and his purpose. You can read that information in the introduction to each book in a good study Bible. I encourage people to read through a book two or three times. (You can probably read Philippians in less than ten minutes.) By the third reading, you begin to notice patterns of thoughts and the thread of the author's reasoning. Then focus on a section at a time—a paragraph or two—to dig deeper into the meaning.

When you study those brief sections, don't rush as if you were checking off an item on your to-do list. Before you begin, ask God to speak to you, and as you study, stop often to ask him for insight. Consider the pattern outlined in Paul's second letter to Timothy.

He wrote, "All Scripture is God-breathed and is useful for teaching, rebuking, correcting and training in righteousness, so that the man of God may be thoroughly equipped for every good work" (2 Timothy 3:16-17). Ask four questions suggested in this passage:

- What does this passage of Scripture teach me about God, about myself, and about life?

- How does my experience fall short of this teaching?

- What changes do I need to make?

- How do I make these changes into new habits?

When we read the Scriptures, and especially the Psalms, we find the honest expression of emotions. It's raw, real-life stuff. The writers tell of their deep disappointment with God, their despair that he hasn't come through the way they hoped he would, and their fear of the threats they face. In almost all cases, though, they come to the conclusion that even in their darkest nights, God is sovereign, he's faithful, and they can trust him.

In addition to your study of Scripture, find women who genuinely pursue God and his truth, and spend time with them. Ask them how they've gained perception about different aspects of their lives, and pay close attention to their answers. Discover how they've trusted God to heal their damaged emotions. Watch them to see how they respond to obstacles and opportunities they face, and emulate their faith.

As you've looked at the principles in this chapter, has anyone come to mind? Who in your life provides the best example of perceptive faith? If someone has been or is currently a model of perception and wisdom for you, take a few minutes to thank her. And become an example for others to follow.

━━━━━━━━━ Healing the Damage ━━━━━━━━━

1. How would you describe someone with clear-eyed faith?

2. Read Colossians 2:2-3. In what way is Christ a treasure trove of wisdom and knowledge?

3. Read 1 Samuel 25. What are some ways we might expect an abused woman to respond in that situation? How did Abigail display wisdom in her response to the crisis?

4. How would living by each of these statements help us grow wise?

   • I belong to God.

   • Every difficult moment and every opportunity is a test designed to strengthen me.

   • I will follow God's leading.

5. Read Romans 12:1-2. What benefits will you receive when God's Word renews your mind?

6. Read 2 Timothy 3:16-17. Do you have a stimulating, effective method of Bible study? If not, try those four questions with a paragraph or two of Scripture and ask God to use your time in the Word to give you more wisdom.

━━━━━━━ Bible Passages on Clear-Eyed Faith ━━━━━━━

"Evil men do not understand justice,
　　but those who seek the LORD understand all things"
　　(Proverbs 28:5).

"You will discern the fear of the LORD
And discover the knowledge of God.
For the LORD gives wisdom;

From His mouth come knowledge and understanding.
He stores up sound wisdom for the upright;
He is a shield to those who walk in integrity"
(Proverbs 2:5-6 NASB).

"We know that the Son of God has come, and has given us understanding so that we may know Him who is true; and we are in Him who is true, in His Son Jesus Christ. This is the true God and eternal life" (1 John 5:20 NASB).

"God, who said, 'Light shall shine out of darkness,' is the One who has shone in our hearts to give the Light of the knowledge of the glory of God in the face of Christ" (2 Corinthians 4:6 NASB).

"If men rise up to pursue you and to seek your life, the life of my lord shall be bound in the bundle of the living in the care of the LORD your God. And the lives of your enemies he shall sling out as from the hollow of a sling. And when the LORD has done to my lord according to all the good that he has spoken concerning you and has appointed you prince over Israel, my lord shall have no cause of grief or pangs of conscience for having shed blood without cause or for my lord taking vengeance himself. And when the LORD has dealt well with my lord, then remember your servant" (1 Samuel 25:29-31 ESV).

"I appeal to you therefore, brothers, by the mercies of God, to present your bodies as a living sacrifice, holy and acceptable to God, which is your spiritual worship. Do not be conformed to this world, but be transformed by the renewal of your mind, that by testing you may discern what is the will of God, what is good and acceptable and perfect" (Romans 12:1-2 ESV).

"All Scripture is breathed out by God and profitable for teaching, for reproof, for correction, and for training in righteousness, that the man of God may be competent, equipped for every good work" (2 Timothy 3:16-17 ESV).

12

*G*od's *D*elight

He brought me out into a broad place;
he rescued me, because he delighted in me.

PSALM 18:19 ESV

I have a friend whose daughter lived in China for several years. Sarah is a tall, pretty blonde. When my friend flew over to visit Sarah, she was amazed at an event that happened repeatedly when they walked down the street together. Raven-haired Chinese girls approached them, giggled, and asked to have their picture taken with Sarah. Quite often, they looked up at Sarah and said admiringly, "You are so beautiful!"

A few seconds after this happened the first time, Sarah and her mom walked down the street a few more paces, and more girls came up to ask for a picture with her. My friend asked her, "What in the world is all this about?"

Sarah just smiled and said, "It's no big deal. They think every blonde is beautiful."

A few years before, when Sarah was in college, a modeling agency came to the campus to look for prospects. As Sarah walked to class one day, a stylish young woman stopped her and said, "I'm with a modeling agency, and you have the look we want. Will you stop by for an interview? I think you have a fabulous future in modeling."

Sarah felt flattered. For a moment, her mind danced with images of her picture on the cover of magazines, but she shook those out of her head and replied, "Thank you very much, but no, I don't think I'm interested."

The value of a statement is in the authority of the speaker. Sarah didn't think much of the adulation of the Chinese girls simply because they said the same thing to any girl who happened to be blonde. But for a modeling agency to say she was beautiful—that was different. Beauty is in the eye of the beholder, and we value a compliment of our beauty if we respect the one who offers it.

Never has physical beauty been so prized as it is today. People have always marveled at a gorgeous figure and a pretty face, but in our contemporary culture, we are bombarded with images of striking women all day, every day. Years ago, women might have compared themselves to the prettiest girl in the nearby farming community or a not-so-dainty model in the Sears catalog, but today, we instinctively compare ourselves to tall, voluptuous beauties on magazine covers and ads, winners and nominees at the Academy Awards, and perhaps most painfully, to the sensuous poses and barely clad beauties in a *Victoria's Secret* catalog or the latest *Sports Illustrated Swimsuit Edition*. On my "fat" days, I feel like taking a swing at one of those models!

Countless women damage their emotions multiple times each day by playing the comparison game with beautiful images in magazines, on television, and in the movies. It's a game they can't win. In fact, even many of these models and movie stars wrestle with feelings of inferiority because they wonder if they're as pretty as someone else or if another year will bring a wrinkle or two and ruin their star status. We may long to look like them, but they live in fear of not measuring up, just like we do.

If we want to know how God sees every aspect of our lives, we can't overlook this crucial point: God's unconditional acceptance of us is very different from the world's system of comparison and competition. People look at the outside, but God peers into our hearts. When God sent the prophet Samuel to Jesse's house to anoint the next king of Israel, Jesse paraded his sons in front of the prophet. They were handsome, big, strong young men. Samuel was impressed with what he saw, and when a singularly fine son stood in front of him, he thought, *Surely this is the one!* But God didn't care about physical beauty. He corrected Samuel: "Do not consider his appearance or his height, for I have rejected him. The LORD does not look at the things man looks at. Man looks at the outward appearance, but the LORD looks at the heart" (1 Samuel 16:7). God directed Samuel to anoint the son who wasn't valued by his father and brothers. The shepherd boy David was to become king of Israel.

Whom does God consider beautiful? He delights in those whose hearts are completely his, who act justly, love mercy, and walk humbly with him. But God's heart also goes out to those who are flawed, those who are considered to be outcasts, and those who are slow to grasp his love—people like you and me.

One of the more striking but overlooked passages in the New Testament depicts a moment on the night Jesus was betrayed. As his followers gathered for their final meal together at Passover, John tells us, "It was just before the Passover Feast. Jesus knew that the time had come for him to leave this world and go to the Father. Having loved his own who were in the world, he now showed them the full extent of his love" (John 13:1). To whom did he show the full extent of his love? To the ones who would run away a couple of hours later when temple guards came to arrest him, to the ones who cowered in fear after he died, to those who had been so slow to grasp who he was and why he came.

How much did he treasure them? So much that he gave himself fully to redeem them. And he values you and me just as much.

Great pieces of art are sold at auction houses in London, New York, or Paris for staggering prices, but people are willing to pay because they treasure these works. God paid a far higher price for you and me. He must consider us supremely valuable, or the Son of God wouldn't have stepped out of the glory of heaven to live, suffer ridicule, and die at the hands of those who hated him—to demonstrate his wondrous love to you and me.

> The most beautiful things in the world cannot be seen or even touched; they must be felt with the heart.
>
> HELEN KELLER

Not So Pretty

The book of Genesis includes a painful story that teaches us a rich lesson about true beauty. Jacob was the younger son of Isaac, but he was a scoundrel. With the help of his mother, he stole his older brother's birthright. When his brother threatened to kill him, Jacob fled to live with his uncle in a foreign land. The uncle had two daughters. The Scriptures tell us: "Leah had weak eyes, but Rachel was lovely in form, and beautiful" (Genesis 29:17). What does "weak eyes" mean? I don't think she just needed glasses. She probably had some kind of protruding eyes or another problem that made her... well, ugly—especially compared to her attractive sister.

From the moment he arrived, Jacob had his eye on the gorgeous younger sister, and he agreed to work for seven years for her hand. But in Jacob's uncle, Laban, he met his match in cunning and deceit. As was the custom of the day, on the wedding night, Jacob got drunk and went in to have sex with his bride. The next morning, he woke up, shook the cobwebs out of his head, and peered over at his wife. To his utter shock, the woman lying beside him was Leah! Jacob jumped up and ran to confront his scheming uncle. Laban explained that it was their custom to marry the older daughter first, but he struck a deal with Jacob. He could have Rachel too if he'd agree to work for him another seven years. Jacob was so stricken with Rachel's beauty that he was willing to agree to anything, so he signed up for another seven years. After a week with Leah, he married his beloved Rachel.

Think about what this must have done to poor Leah. Every day, she watched her husband fawn over her beautiful sister. Jacob's attention to Rachel must have stabbed Leah's heart over and over again. She felt ugly, unloved, and unwanted. But God had something to teach her. Amid her pain, Leah naturally longed for her husband's affection. When she had a son, she named him Reuben, and she said, "It is because the LORD has seen my misery. Surely my husband will love me now." But he didn't. When she had a second son, Leah remarked, "Because the LORD heard that I am not loved, he gave me this one too." And after a third son, her hopes were still strong. She said, "Now at last my husband will become attached to me, because I have borne him three sons." But Jacob's heart was still firmly attached to Rachel.

The pain must have been excruciating, but Leah's perspective began to change. She realized that her hope, her joy, and her delight couldn't be found in a man whose eyes were on someone else. She learned to see herself as beautiful in God's eyes. When she had her fourth son, she remarked, "This time I will praise the LORD" (Genesis 29:31-35).

The story of God's delight, though, doesn't end there. The fourth son was named Judah. When we look at the rest of Scripture, we find that the Messiah was called "the Lion of Judah." Jesus came from the tribe of Judah, so the hope of the world was traced back to Leah, not Rachel. The important lesson is that God turns beauty upside down. He loves every person—beautiful, plain, or ugly—but we find over and over in the Scriptures that God takes extraordinary delight in showing his favor to women the world considers expendable.

Beauty is when you look into a woman's
eyes and see what is in her heart.
NATE DIRCKS

====== Fresh Insights ======

How much of our time is spent trying to look more beautiful so we can become acceptable? I'm certainly not suggesting we forsake taking care of ourselves, but I recommend that we take a good, hard look at how obsessed we may be with beauty. Instead of inflicting more emotional damage on ourselves every time we look at a magazine or glance in the mirror, we can be certain that God cherishes us and delights in us just as we are. Comparing ourselves with others—in the media or in the grocery store—robs us of peace and perspective, and we need God's gentle correction.

Even if others don't treasure us, God does. Even if those who made solemn commitments to value us have failed in those commitments to some degree, God never fails to hold us in highest esteem. Like Jesus' love for his often confused disciples, God's love for us isn't conditioned on us being something we're not. He loves us for who we are, and that kind of love transforms us from the inside out. As our hearts bask in his tender and strong love, our eyes begin to show it. Hard lines of worry and resentment soften, and the glare of defensiveness turns into the look of kindness and confidence.

At a crucial point in the nation of Israel, the people turned their backs on God and suffered the consequences of captivity. Even there, God didn't abandon them. In a beautiful statement of God's gracious intentions toward them, the prophet Isaiah quotes God:

> But now, this is what the LORD says—
> he who created you, O Jacob,
> he who formed you, O Israel:
> "Fear not, for I have redeemed you;
> I have summoned you by name; you are mine.
> When you pass through the waters,
> I will be with you;
> and when you pass through the rivers,
> they will not sweep over you.
> When you walk through the fire,

you will not be burned;
the flames will not set you ablaze.
For I am the LORD, your God,
The Holy One of Israel, your Savior;
I give Egypt for your ransom,
Cush and Seba in your stead" (Isaiah 43:1-3).

God never promises that we won't experience disappointments and problems, but he assures us that we belong to him regardless of what happens. The most often quoted command in the Bible is "fear not." In this passage, God reminds Israel that he is in their midst and will be with them always. The same is true for us. We will experience the full range of human joys and trials, but through them all, he is there.

In the New Testament letters, Paul reminds us over and over again of God's undying devotion to us. He tells us we are accepted in the One he loves, that God's love is higher, deeper, wider, and longer than we can imagine, and that he has equipped us to join him in touching others' lives (Ephesians 1:5-6; 2:10; 3:18). In his letter to the believers in Rome, Paul goes to great lengths to correct their thinking and calm their fears. In a series of questions and answers in chapter 8, he speaks boldly to fears of being unlovable, to doubts about our value, and to concerns that God might give up on us. After explaining God's grand and glorious purpose for his children, he asks, "What, then, shall we say in response to this? If God is for us, who can be against us?" He answers with a searching question that stirs our souls: "He who did not spare his own Son, but gave him up for us all—how will he not also, along with him, graciously give us all things?" (Romans 8:31-32). In other words, if God was willing to give his Son to die for us, he is obviously deeply, completely, and tenderly devoted to us all day every day. The cross is the ultimate measure of God's commitment to us, and when we think of it, we are assured of his unmeasured affection. We are beautiful to him.

Taking joy in living is a woman's best cosmetic.
ROSALIND RUSSELL

Steps Forward

"Tim, how do I look?" That's a question I ask him every day, whether I actually say it or not. (He's learned how to answer.) The truth is that God sees us as his beloved every day! We may seem plain on the outside, but God sees our inward beauty. Here are three recommendations that can help you experience more of his delight in you.

Capture your thoughts.

A mark of spiritual maturity is the ability to examine our thoughts to determine whether they are worthy, healthy, and God honoring. Comparison kills. It consumes our mental activity, poisons our desires, and robs us of joy. How long can a woman enjoy life when she wonders, *I'm not as pretty as she is,* or *I'm not as smart as she is,* or *I'm not in the same crowd she is in,* or *I'm not as popular as she is?*

For a bit of practice, examine the thoughts you've had today. What were they and how did they affect you? How much time did you spend comparing yourself (favorably or unfavorably) to someone else, feeling sorry for yourself because you don't measure up to an external standard of success or beauty, or blaming others for getting in the way or not giving you the praise you think you deserve? How much time did you spend looking at beautiful people in stories or advertisements in magazines and on television? And how much time did you spend thanking God for his grace toward you?

Choose the voice you listen to.

We don't have to passively accept the messages that the media, our friends, or our family members send our way. We can choose which voices to listen to, which to carefully consider, and which to ignore. These voices speak to us not only through what we hear but also through what we see. Think carefully about the messages that come into your mind and heart, and choose to fill your soul with God's perception of true beauty. This commitment, I assure you, will require a real fight, so expect to face stern opposition—perhaps from some of your closest friends who remain committed to chasing the empty dream of acceptance through physical beauty.

Delight in God's love and acceptance.

Do you sometimes feel like Leah? At the core of your being, are you convinced that you are ugly and unacceptable? Leah had every reason to believe her husband did not accept her. His attention was firmly fixed on her beautiful sister. Leah longed for his affection, but his daily preference for Rachel must have nearly broken her heart. Like all of us, she had to find true meaning in life apart from physical beauty or the affection of a man. She had to find it in God.

Is God delightful to you today? Do you sense that he's crazy about you, that he loves you with a powerful, tender affection? That's the picture we get from the Scriptures. If you are a gorgeous woman, don't let your physical beauty define who you are. Go deeper, beyond skin deep, to find true beauty in your relationship with God. And if you feel a bit on the plain side, stop comparing yourself with every woman who walks past you each day. Arrest your thoughts and focus your heart on God's undying affection for you.

As a woman, this is easy to say, but oh, so hard to do! You know how tough it can be to rest in God's delight. One day, you're fine. You know that God loves you. You feel it. *I am a beautiful creation of God*, you tell yourself. The next day, your confidence comes crashing down simply because of a coworker, a catalog, or an advertisement on TV. Thoughts that you're ugly or fat come rushing back, and you seriously doubt that *anyone* could ever delight in you. You burn dinner, act short with the kids, and fall into bed feeling like an utter failure. "No one could ever love me," you mutter in exhaustion.

Let me encourage you, my sister, to soak your heart and mind in the truth of God's love for you. He is not fickle, like some guys who might have said "I love you." His love for you is perfect. Fight the *He loves me not* thoughts in your head with the truth of the Bible: *He loves me*. Period. No ifs, ands, or buts. Settle it! Anchored to the unchangeable love of Jesus you are secure.

As you considered this chapter on God's delight in you, did you think of someone who needs this reminder? Do you know someone who is so filled with God's love that her countenance proclaims, "I'm deeply loved and fully accepted. God delights in me!" I hope you know someone like that, and even more, I hope you become that person.

=== Healing the Damage ===

1. How do you feel when you delight someone you respect?

2. Read Genesis 29:15-30. How would you feel if you were Leah on the morning after her wedding? How would you feel every day watching Jacob focus his desires on your sister?

3. Read Genesis 29:31-35. Describe Leah's hope after she had her first three sons. What do you think happened in her heart that helped her to praise God when Judah was born?

4. What is the danger of comparing yourself with others? How much do comparisons affect you personally?

5. Read Isaiah 43:1-3 and Romans 8:32-39. What do these passages tell you about God's devotion to you?

6. Take a few minutes now to...

   Capture your thoughts.

   Choose the voice you listen to.

   Delight in God's love for you.

"Now before the Feast of the Passover, when Jesus knew that his hour had come to depart out of this world to the Father, having loved his own who were in the world, he loved them to the end" (John 13:1 ESV).

"When the LORD saw that Leah was hated, he opened her womb, but Rachel was barren. And Leah conceived and bore a son, and she called his name Reuben, for she said, 'Because the LORD has looked upon my affliction; for now my husband will love me.' She conceived again and bore a son, and said, 'Because the LORD has heard that I am hated, he has given me this son also.' And she called his name Simeon. Again she conceived and bore a son, and said, 'Now this time my husband will be attached to me, because I have borne him three sons.' Therefore his name was called Levi. And she conceived again and bore a son, and said, 'This time I will praise the LORD.' Therefore she called his name Judah. Then she ceased bearing" (Genesis 29:31-35 ESV).

"Paul, an apostle of Christ Jesus by the will of God, to the saints who are in Ephesus, and are faithful in Christ Jesus: Grace to you and peace from God our Father and the Lord Jesus Christ.

"Blessed be the God and Father of our Lord Jesus Christ, who has blessed us in Christ with every spiritual blessing in the heavenly places, even as he chose us in him before the foundation of the world, that we should be holy and blameless before him. In love he predestined us for adoption as sons through Jesus Christ, according to the purpose of his will, to the praise of his glorious grace, with which he has blessed us in the Beloved. In him we have redemption through his blood, the forgiveness of our trespasses, according to the riches of his grace, which he lavished upon us, in all wisdom and insight making known to us the mystery of his will, according to his purpose, which he set forth in Christ as a plan for the fullness of time, to unite all things in him, things in heaven and things on earth" (Ephesians 1:1-10 ESV).

"I bow my knees before the Father, from whom every family in heaven and on earth is named, that according to the riches of his glory he may grant you to be strengthened with power through his Spirit in your inner being, so that Christ may dwell in your hearts through faith—that you, being rooted and grounded in love, may have strength to comprehend with all the saints what is the breadth and length and height and depth, and to know the love of Christ that surpasses knowledge, that you may be filled with all the fullness of God" (Ephesians 3:14-19 ESV).

"For we are his workmanship, created in Christ Jesus for good works, which God prepared beforehand, that we should walk in them" (Ephesians 2:10 ESV).

13

A New Day—a New You

Love comes to those who still hope even though
they've been disappointed, to those who still believe
even though they've been betrayed, to those who
still love even though they've been hurt before.

ANONYMOUS

For more than a year, I watched as the expression on Janet's face changed from confusion to confidence. It was a remarkable transition.

I first met her when she asked for a few minutes to talk about her relationship with her husband, Tony. After only a few seconds, I knew we needed much more time to explore the depths of their troubled marriage. Over coffee the next morning, she told me that she should have seen it when they were dating, but she had minimized his drinking and his wandering eye. Only a few days before we talked that morning, she had stumbled across a note from his lover. For years, she had suspected he was unfaithful, but he always turned her accusations around by saying that for her to think he was committing adultery must come from her guilt because she was unfaithful. Then, instead of finding truth, she was instantly on the defensive.

As she explained to me the pain and confusion she had endured for so long, she had a blank stare. I asked if she felt like crying or screaming, but she simply told me, "No, I've cried a river of tears.

I'm cried out." We talked about being objective about Tony and their marriage, and she blurted out, "Julie, I've been living a lie for 12 years!"

Janet saw a counselor and attended a support group during the next year. With the strength and clarity of mind she received from those who had been down the same road before, she confronted Tony on several occasions. Sometimes he exploded in rage, but a couple of times he wept and said he was sorry. Still, he never stopped seeing the other woman. Finally, Janet drew a line in the sand and told him to make his choice. He did. He packed up, leaving her and their three young children.

Facing reality required courage, but Janet had found the strength to speak the truth and offer Tony reconciliation if he'd take steps back toward the relationship. Now, with Tony's hurtful rejection of her offer, Janet felt completely alone. But she wasn't. Her counselor and friends continued to give her lots of support, and with their help, she began to carve out a new life after the divorce. Gradually, the look of confusion changed to anger, then to sadness, and finally to renewed confidence that God loves her dearly and has a wonderful purpose for her life.

Today, Janet is one of the most delightful women I know. The joy in her eyes is tempered from time to time by looks of pained compassion as she helps other women who are walking through troubled relationships. She has found her calling. I've heard people say that the pains of our past provide a platform for our present ministry. I've seen this dynamic at work countless times, including in Janet's life.

The Scriptures are completely honest about every aspect of life— no rose-colored glasses and no impenetrable clouds of doom. We would do well to follow their guidance. Deception is all around us, but God calls us to wipe away the film from our eyes so that we see clearly. Only then can we respond appropriately to every answered prayer, every test of our faith, and every gift of love.

Joy is the holy fire that keeps our purpose
warm and our hearts aglow.
HELEN KELLER

Mary's Objectivity

Some Christian traditions give a lot of attention to Jesus' mother, and others tend to discount her role in the narrative of faith. But Mary was a remarkable woman who trusted God in the most difficult circumstances imaginable. She was probably a young teenager when the angel Gabriel appeared to her to inform her that she had been chosen by God to bear the promised Messiah. With a remarkably clear mind, she instantly realized the implications, and she asked, "How can this be, since I am a virgin?" (Luke 1:34)

The angel explained that the Holy Spirit would come to her and overshadow her. This would be like no other conception the world has ever known and will ever know, for Mary would become pregnant with the Son of God. She replied to that mind-boggling explanation in humble faith: "I am the Lord's servant…May it be to me as you have said."

Has there ever been a girl in such a delicate, difficult, threatening position? She could count on almost no one believing her story. She could expect to be branded as an adulterer. How would her fiancé respond? Would he understand, or would he reject her? In spite of these immense obstacles, Mary persisted in believing God, trusting him to guide her, protect her, and see her through.

And God paved the way for her. She gave birth in a cattle stall many miles from her home, and God confirmed the truth the angel had spoken nine months before as a myriad of angels sang praises to God in the sky. Shepherds in the fields that night ran to the stable to see the child the angels sang about. When they walked in, they worshipped the little baby. Mary, always combining clear-eyed objectivity with faith, took in the moment. Luke tells us, "But Mary treasured up all these things and pondered them in her heart" (Luke 2:19).

The Gospel accounts provide only fleeting glimpses of the years before Jesus picked his disciples and began his ministry, but we can imagine what life must have been like as Mary watched God's chosen Messiah grow up under her roof. And when Jesus began traveling and proclaiming the message of the kingdom, Mary often followed him. Imagine what was in her heart as she watched him perform miracles. She must have almost burst with pride! But imagine as well how she must have felt as she watched people ridicule him mercilessly. Their anger and bitter accusations must have pierced her heart.

If I had been in her sandals, I would have wanted to jump in to defend him, protect him, and control the situation. Any mother would want to do that for her son! But we never see Mary interfering in any way. She must have understood that responses to her son the Messiah would include the full range, from marvelous faith to bitter recriminations. And she must have eventually understood that she would have to watch as her beloved son suffered and died for her and for us all to forgive our sins.

Mary is a wonderful example of trusting God through difficulties, threats, and rejection. She didn't have a formal education, and she probably never studied philosophy or theology, but she lived in the intersection of visible reality and strong faith in an unseen God. Her responses, from Gabriel's first appearance in her room to Jesus' ascension into heaven, provide a model for us as we too try to live in that intersection.

> Promise me you'll always remember: You're braver than you believe, and stronger than you seem, and smarter than you think.
>
> A.A. MILNE

Fresh Insights

A woman's walk in faith is a combination of certainty and mystery. The journey is based on the bedrock of history described in the Bible, including the earliest days of the patriarchs, the establishment of the nation of Israel, God's gracious restoration of the nation when they sinned (time after time), the accounts of the life of Christ, and the early years of the church. But we live for someone we can't see, a God who created all that exists but whose glory remains at least partly obscured because we'd die if we actually saw him in all of his majesty.

In a wonderful and poignant description of a faith-filled life, Paul compares his body to a jar of clay that holds the treasure of Christ (2 Corinthians 4:7). We, the messengers of eternal truth, are all too mortal, fragile, and plain. God wants us to look at life through two sets of lenses: our physical eyes and our spiritual eyes. As we walk the earth, we must avoid seeing only what we want to see and ignoring facts that seem inconvenient or threatening.

When David considered that God knows everything, sees everything, and is present everywhere at all times, he responded by inviting God to show him the deepest truths in his life. He prayed, "Search me, O God, and know my heart; test me and know my anxious thoughts. See if there is any offensive way in me, and lead me in the way everlasting" (Psalm 139:23-24). David was asking God to show him cracks in his clay jar, big gashes that everybody notices and hairline cracks that no one else sees. When I've prayed that prayer, God has answered. Sometimes, God reminds me of a conversation I had with Tim, my children, or a friend in which I was less than kind or stretched the truth a bit to make a point. Sometimes God shines his light on a hidden desire that makes him unhappy. I may have thought the desire was completely justified because "everyone's doing it," but God wanted to purify my deepest motives.

No one said it's easy to be completely honest about the realities of life and trust God in the middle of every moment. Paul acknowledges how tough it is to hold the real and the ideal in our hearts at the same time. This is his strategy:

> We do not lose heart. Though outwardly we are wasting away, yet inwardly we are being renewed day by day. For our light and momentary troubles are achieving for us

an eternal glory that far outweighs them all. So we fix
our eyes not on what is seen, but on what is unseen. For
what is seen is temporary, but what is unseen is eternal
(2 Corinthians 4:16-18).

If we look only at what is seen with our physical eyes, we can
easily become discouraged, and doubts cloud our hearts. But if our
spiritual eyes become clear and strong, we'll cling to God through
thick and thin, trusting him to accomplish his will (not necessarily ours) in every situation. We'll have his perspective about the
struggles of life, knowing in the depths of our hearts that God is
using every moment of every day to shape us, prepare us, and use
us to touch others around us.

Paul reminds us that our true hope reaches far beyond today and
into eternity. When our eyes get a glimpse of eternal glory, our perspective on today's challenges changes focus. We no longer feel compelled to escape problems or control people. Instead, we realize that
this life is a proving ground for eternity. That's why Paul could respond
in his letter to the Philippians about the searing problems he faced
with the seemingly offhand comment, "To live is Christ, and to die
is gain" (Philippians 1:21). All that matters in this life is that Christ
is honored. Not our comfort, not our affluence, and not the acclaim
of others—only that Jesus is in the spotlight so that people know
him and love him. But we're assured that a day will come when we'll
see Jesus "up close and personal," when all things will be made right.
Problems that confused us now will make perfect sense, and we'll see
how God's hand was at work even in the most difficult situations in
our lives. With clear vision for our physical eyes and our spiritual eyes,
we embrace both certainty and mystery, and the unknowns of life no
longer scare us. Mystery confuses some of us because it makes us feel
out of control. We can be confident, however, that God is always in
control, accomplishing far more than we can imagine. Author Dennis Covington wrote, "Mystery is not the absence of meaning, but
the presence of more meaning than we can comprehend."

Steps Forward

Reclaiming our lives takes much more than a few minutes of surgery. It requires a lifetime of reflection, courage, and conversation. Just as Mary pondered events in her heart to gain God's insights about significant moments in her life, we can do the same with the events of our lives. Instead of rushing from one activity to another with barely a moment in between, we can create space in our schedules for quiet so we can think and pray. Does that sound hard to do? Of course it is! It goes against our nature and our culture, but it's essential if we are to live in truth.

Like David, we need to pray regularly, "Search me, O God, and know my heart; test me and know my anxious thoughts. See if there is any offensive way in me, and lead me in the way everlasting" (Psalm 139:23-24)—and then listen. Quite often, the Holy Spirit takes this opportunity to show us something instantly, but other insights take a little longer. Perhaps he has to prepare our hearts so we'll listen, or maybe he wants to shine his light on a hidden motive that has remained buried for many years. The invitation to ask God to search us, though, doesn't have to be terrifying. God is a gracious, forgiving, patient God. We can trust him to lead us where he wants us to go, to forgive the offenses where he shines his light, and to heal the wounds he uncovers.

The journey of reclaiming our lives isn't one we undertake alone. We don't need a crowd to go with us, but we need a few people—maybe only one. God has made us for relationships with him and with other people. We all have blind spots, and we need a trusted friend to point those out to us. We all want to quit from time to time, so we need a friend who will walk with us through the darkness and back into the light.

As our faith becomes stronger, we'll be more perceptive of changes we need to make—changes in our words, our attitudes, and our actions. But we also need to make changes in our priorities to value time with God and be in his Word. We need time to fill our minds with grace and truth so we can stand strong against devilish schemes and cultural deceptions.

Embrace both certainty and mystery. Recognize the reality of each situation, but also cling to your confidence that God is far above all, beyond anything we can imagine. His wisdom is as deep as the ocean, and his love as high as the heavens. We simply can't grasp all that he is. In response to his greatness, we bow and worship.

In the opening chapter, we looked at Paul's prayer in his letter to the Ephesians; let's go back to it now. His two-thousand-year-old prayer for them is my prayer for us today as we try to live in clear-eyed faith:

> I keep asking that the God of our Lord Jesus Christ, the glorious Father, may give you the Spirit of wisdom and revelation, so that you may know him better. I pray also that the eyes of your heart may be enlightened in order that you may know the hope to which he has called you, the riches of his glorious inheritance in the saints, and his incomparably great power for us who believe (Ephesians 1:17-19).

Get rid of the bondage and live free. God's grace and strength can liberate you from your past and equip and empower you to help other women (2 Corinthians 1:2-4). Whose life needs to be reclaimed from the wreckage of damaged emotions? As you experience healing, reach out to the other women in your life to share the hope you've found. To make it through this life, and handle our at-times crazy emotions, we need each other!

Do you know some women, maybe just one or two, who are deeply committed to authenticity in their own lives, their relationships with people, and their relationship with God? I hope you know at least one person like that, and I hope you feel deeply motivated to become that kind of person. Your life will change with every step you take as the eyes of your heart are enlightened by God's grace and truth.

Friendship is born at that moment when one person says
to another, "What! You too? I thought I was the only one!"

C.S. LEWIS

Healing the Damage

1. Who is the most objective woman you know? What
   are some of the benefits of objectivity in her life? Is
   that attractive to you, scary to you, or offensive to you?
   Explain your answer.

2. Read Luke 1:26-38. What are some ways Mary
   demonstrates perception and faith in her encounter
   with the angel?

3. Read Luke 2:8-20 and John 19:25-27. What do you
   think it was like for Mary to be objective about all that
   happened to her son?

4. Read 2 Corinthians 4:16-18. Paraphrase this passage.
   What does Paul mean when he says, "We fix our eyes
   not on what is seen, but on what is unseen"?

5. Take a few minutes now to pray David's prayer at
   the end of Psalm 139 and Paul's prayer in Ephesians
   1—and take time to listen.

6. What are two or three of the most significant insights
   you've gained from this book? What are some ways those
   insights can become even more a reality in your life?

Bible Passages on a New Day and a New You

"From now on, therefore, we regard no one according to the flesh. Even though we once regarded Christ according to the flesh, we regard him thus no longer. Therefore, if anyone is in Christ, he is a new creation. The old has passed away; behold, the new has come. All this is from God who through Christ reconciled us to himself and gave us the ministry of reconciliation" (2 Corinthians 5:16-18 ESV).

"But you are a chosen race, a royal priesthood, a holy nation, a people for God's own possession, so that you may proclaim the excellencies of Him who has called you out of darkness into His marvelous light; for you once were not a people, but now you are the people of God; you had not received mercy, but now you have received mercy" (1 Peter 2:9-10 NASB).

"So then you are no longer strangers and aliens, but you are fellow citizens with the saints, and are of God's household" (Ephesians 2:19 NASB).

"We are ambassadors for Christ" (2 Corinthians 5:20 NASB).

"Having been freed from sin, you became slaves of righteousness" (Romans 6:18 NASB).

"Let your eyes look directly ahead
And let your gaze be fixed straight in front of you.
Watch the path of your feet
And all your ways will be established.
Do not turn to the right nor to the left;
Turn your foot from evil" (Proverbs 4:25-27 NASB).

"Trust in the LORD with all your heart
And do not lean on your own understanding.
In all your ways acknowledge Him,

And He will make your paths straight"
(Proverbs 3:5-6 NASB).

"So we do not lose heart. Though our outer nature is wasting away, our inner nature is being renewed day by day. For this slight momentary affliction is preparing for us an eternal weight of glory beyond all comparison, as we look not to the things that are seen but to the things that are unseen. For the things that are seen are transient, but the things that are unseen are eternal" (2 Corinthians 4:16-18 ESV).

Notes

Introduction: Windows into a Woman's Heart

1. people.howstuffworks.com/framed.htm?parent=women.htm&url=http://www.galluppoll. com/content/?ci=1978&pg=1.

2. people.howstuffworks.com/framed.htm?parent=women.htm&url=http://select.nytimes.com/ gst/abstract.html?res=F70B15FF3C5B0C708DDDA90994DD404482.

3. N.T. Wright, *Following Jesus* (Grand Rapids: Eerdman's, 1994), 113.

Chapter 1: Anxious and Afraid

1. Linda Lyons, "What Frightens America's Youth?" *Gallup*, March 25, 2009. www.gallup.com/ poll/15439/what-frightens-americas-youth.aspx.

2. David Dishneau, "AP: DC Sniper Execution Causes Fear." *Sweetness & Light*, November 9, 2009. sweetness-light.com/archive/ap-dc-area-relives-muhammad-terror.

3. Merle Shain, *Some Men Are More Perfect than Others* (New York: Bantam, 1984).

Chapter 2: Hurt: How Pain Steals Our Joy

1. See "Domestic Violence Is a Serious, Widespread Social Problem in America: The Facts," *Adoption.com*, www.library.adoption.com/articles/domestic-violence-is-a-serious-widespread-social-problem-in-america-the-facts.html. See also C.J. Newton, "Child Abuse: An Overview," *Findcounseling.com*, www.therapistfinder.net/Child-Abuse/Child-Abuse-Statistics.html.

2. "An Overview of Abortion in the Unites States," *The Guttmacher Institute*, www.guttmacher. org/media/presskits/2005/06/28/abortionoverview.html.

3. American Psychological Association, "Briefing Sheet: Women and Depression," *APA Online*, www.apa.org/ppo/issues/pwomenanddepress.html.

4. Regarding irritable bowel syndrome, see "Statistics about Irritable Bowel Syndrome," *Cure Research.com*, May 30, 2003, www.cureresearch.com/i/irritable_bowel_syndrome/stats.htm. Regarding eating disorders, see "Statistics on Eating Disorders," *Anne Collins Weight Loss Program 2009*, www.annecollins.com/eating-disorders/statistics.htm.

5. Ernest Becker, *The Denial of Death* (New York: Free Press, 1973), 284.

6. Dallas Willard, *The Spirit of Disciplines: Understanding How God Changes Lives* (San Francisco: Harper and Row, 1988), viii.

7. Dan Allender, *The Healing Path* (Colorado Springs: Waterbrook Press, 1999), 5-6.

Chapter 3: The Flame of Anger

1. "Intermittent Explosive Disorder Affects up to 16 Million Americans." National Institute of Mental Health press release, June, 2006. www.nimh.nih.gov/science-news/2006/intermittent-explosive-disorder-affects-up-to-16-million-americans.shtml.

2. Karen S. Peterson, "Why Everyone Is So Short-Tempered," USA Today, July 18, 2000.

3. "Rage: Dr. Frank Farley," USA Today.com live chat, July 18, 2001. www.usatoday.com/community/chat/0718farley.htm.

4. "ABC News Poll: Minding Your Manners," May 17, 1999. abcnews.go.com/images/pdf/791a1Manners.pdf.

5. Ibid.

6. "Integra Realty Resources: Is America Suffering from 'Desk Rage?' Fights and Yelling Are Common as Layoffs and Contracting Economy Put Stress on American Workers," BNET, December 13, 2001. findarticles.com/p/articles/mi_m0EIN/is_2001_Dec_13/ai_80763905/?tag=content;col1.

7. S. Barsade, B. Wiesenfeld, and the Marlin Company. "Attitudes in the American workplace III," Unpublished manuscript, Yale University School of Management, 1997.

8. G. Namie and R. Namie, "Beware of Bullies at Work," *The Intelligencer Journal,* October 31, 2002.

9. D. Connell and M. Joint, "Aggressive Driving: Three Studies." AAA Foundation for Traffic Safety, 1997, 27-36.

10. "Aggressive Driving and the Law: A Symposium." National Highway Traffic Safety Administration, May, 1999.

11. Tim Dahlberg, "Sideline rage: Violence in youth sports spreading." Associated Press Archive, June 2, 2001.

12. C. Puzzanchera, "Juvenile Justice Bulletin—Juvenile Arrests in 2007," U.S. Department of Justice, Office of Juvenile Justice and Delinquency Prevention, April 2009. http://www.ncjrs.gov/pdffiles1/ojjdp/225344.pdf.

13. H.N. Snyder and M. Sickmund, "Juvenile offenders and victims: 1999 national report," Office of Juvenile Justice and Delinquency Prevention, 1999, 26.

14. "The Ethics of American Youth: 2008," Josephson Institute Center for Youth Ethics, 2008. charactercounts.org/programs/reportcard/2008/index.html.

15. D. Finkelhor, K. Mitchell, and J. Wolak, "Online Victimization: A Report on the Nation's Youth," National Center for Missing and Exploited Children, June 2000. www.missingkids.com/en_US/publications/NC62.pdf.

16. Dr. Nancy Nason-Clark, "When Terror Strikes the Christian Home," keynote address at The Awakening Conference, Ft. Lauderdale, October 7, 2006.

17. For more information about efforts to stop the sex slave trade, go to www.Love146.org or notforsalecampaign.org.

18. Lewis B. Smedes, "Forgiveness: The Power to Change the Past," *Christianity Today,* January 7, 1983.

Chapter 4: Depression

1. *Diagnostic and Statistical Manual of Mental Disorders,* fourth edition (Washington DC: American Psychiatric Association, 2000), 372.

2. M.W. O'Hara and A.M. Swain, "Rates and risk of postpartum depression: A meta-analysis," *International Review of Psychiatry,* 1996, 8:37-54.

3. E.K. Moscicki, "Epidemiology of completed and attempted suicide: toward a framework for prevention," *Clinical Neuroscience Research,* 2001, 1:310-23.

4. *Diagnostic and Statistical Manual of Mental Disorders,* 356-62.

5. O'Hara and Swain, 37-54.

6. M.A. Whisman, "Marital adjustment and outcome following treatments for depression," *Journal of Consulting and Clinical Psychology,* 2001, 69:125-129.

7. T.A. Grady-Weliky, "Premenstrual dysphoric disorder," *New England Journal of Medicine,* 2003, 348(5): 433-37.

Chapter 5: Lust: Never Enough Love

1. Excerpt taken from John Piper's sermon "Battling the Unbelief of Lust," DesiringGod.org, November 13, 1988. www.desiringgod.org/ResourceLibrary/Sermons/ByDate/1988/657_Battling_the_Unbelief_of_Lust.

2. Jerry Ropelato, "Internet Pornography Statistics," *Internet Filter Software Review,* 2006. www.internet-filter-review.toptenreviews.com/internet-pornography-statistics.html.

3. Meghan Daum, "The recession heats up romance novels," *Los Angeles Times,* April 4, 2009.

4. Ropelato.

5. "About the Romance Genre," *Romance Writers of America,* www.rwanational.org/cs/readership_stats.

6. Visit www.faithfulandtrueministries.com and see Doug Rosenau, *A Celebration of Sex: A Guide to Enjoying God's Gift of Sexual Intimacy* (Nashville: Thomas Nelson, 2002); Clifford Penner and Joyce Penner, *The Gift of Sex: A Guide to Sexual Fulfillment* (Nashville: Thomas Nelson, 2003); Shaunti Feldhahn, *For Women Only* (Sisters, OR: Multnomah Books, 2004).

Chapter 6: Envy and Jealousy

1. Frederick C. Miner, Jr. "Jealousy on the Job," *Personnel Journal,* April 2000.

Chapter 8: Stressed and Exhausted

1. The first four bullet points are adapted from Kate Lorenz, "5 Signs of Job Burnout...and What to Do About It," *CareerBuilder.com,* February 17, 2009.

2. U.S. Bureau of Labor, "Current Population Survey," *America's Children: Key National Indicators of Well-Being,* www.childstats.gov/americaschildren/surveys2.asp#cps,

3. Holmes and Rahe Stress Scale, cited in Robert M. Kaplan and Dennis P. Saccuzzo, *Psychological Testing: Principles, Applications, and Issues* (Pacific Grove: Brooks/Cole Publishing, 1989), 445-47.

4. "Economy and Money Top Causes of Stress for Americans," *American Psychological Association,* June 4, 2008. www.apa.org/news/press/releases/2008/06/economy-stress.aspx.

5. Dr. Richard Swenson, *Margin: Restoring Emotional, Physical, Financial and Time Reserves to Our Overloaded Lives* (Colorado Springs, NavPress, 2004).

6. Quoted in Martha Irvine, "A generation obsessed with having more stuff," *The Houston Chronicle,* January 23, 2007.

7. lindastone.net/qa/continuous-partial-attention.

8. www.money-zine.com/Financial-Planning/Debt-Consolidation/Credit-Card-Debt-Statistics.

9. "Women and Sleep," *National Sleep Foundation*, www.sleepfoundation.org/article/sleep-topics/women-and-sleep.

Chapter 9: Deep Pain

1. T. Hart and C. Rennison, "Reporting Crime to the Police, 1992-2000," U.S. Department of Justice, Office of Justice Programs, March, 2003.

2. "Who are the victims—Breakdown by Gender and Age" *Rape, Abuse & Incest National Network,* www.rainn.org/get-information/statistics/sexual-assault-victims.

3. Judith Lewis Herman, *Trauma and Recovery* (New York: Basic Books, 1992).

4. Natalie quoted this at the Thirty-sixth Gospel Music Awards in 2005. The couple who lost the child are friends of the song writer, Krista Wells. www.cmcentral.com/news/3562.html.

10. Blind Spots: Eyes Wide Shut

1. Philip Yancey, *Reaching for the Invisible God* (Grand Rapids: Zondervan, 2000), 69.

About the Author

*J*ulie Clinton, M.Ad., M.B.A., is president of Extraordinary Women and host of Extraordinary Women conferences all across America. A woman of deep faith, she cares passionately about seeing women live out their dreams by finding their freedom in Christ. Julie and her husband, Tim, live in Virginia with their children, Megan and Zach.

Julie taught elementary school for five years and later became the executive director of the Liberty Godparent Home, a home for unwed teen mothers. Julie is the author of *Extraordinary Women, Living God's Dream for You,* and *10 Things You Aren't Telling Him,* all published by Harvest House Publishers.

In moments of downtime, which occur less often than desired, Julie enjoys shopping with her daughter and cheering her son on to victory in his many sports events. When she is not at the mall, a basketball game, a football game, or a baseball game, you'll find Julie nestled at home with her new Chihuahua, Simba, enjoying a good cup of coffee.

Extraordinary Women

Extraordinary Women is America's explosive women's movement, drawing women closer to the heart of Jesus. Featuring 16 regional conferences all over America, Extraordinary Women seeks to equip and empower women of all ages through biblical teaching and pure worship experiences. In 2009, more than 100,000 women gathered across the country to be encouraged, equipped, and empowered in their walk with God.

Each Extraordinary Women conference is bursting with real and relevant messages from dynamic speakers such as Angela Thomas, Chonda Pierce, Lysa TerKurst, Stormie Omartian, and Karen Kingsbury, along with incredible worship led by artists such as Mandisa, Newsong, Charles Billingsley, Jeremy Camp, Mathew West, and many more.

Extraordinary Women is not just an event...it's a lifestyle. Now in its eighth year, Extraordinary Women is in touch with women daily to enrich their lives regardless of their religious affiliation. Extraordinary Women encourages and empowers women through weekend conferences, weekly devotionals, a quarterly magazine, and numerous devotional books.

The vision of Extraordinary Women was birthed from the American Association of Christian Counselors. With nearly 50,000 active members, the AACC is committed to assisting Christian counselors and the entire "community of care"—licensed professionals, pastors, and caring church members with little or no formal training. The president of AACC, Dr. Tim Clinton, and the entire AACC staff equip clinical, pastoral, and lay caregivers with biblical truth and counseling insights that offer hope to hurting persons and helps them move to personal wholeness, interpersonal competence, mental stability, and spiritual maturity.

The AACC currently offers a women's ministry leader's certificate of completion program entitled Extraordinary Women. This 31-hour course features presentations from prominent women's leaders such as Beth Moore, Kay Arthur, Jon Erickson Tada, Thelma Wells, Diane Langberg, and Linda Mintle. For more information, visit www.ewomen.net.